Petroleum Exploration

By

Roshdy Ebrahim ,Ph.D

Roshdy Ebrahim

Copyright © 2018 Roshdy Ebrahim

All right reserved

ISBN: 9781980558064

preface

A new era of oil exploration began. Look for salt domes and drill their tops! Any mound on the Gulf Coast was suspect of an underlying salt dome. Many domes were discovered, but only a few produced oil from the cap rock. It was 13 years before oil was first found on the flanks of a piercement dome, at Humble in 1914, and it wasn't until 1925-24 years after the Spindletop discovery-that Frank Yount found oil on its flanks where the Frio sands pinch out against the dome.

In fact, an expert commission of geologists had concluded (back in 1871) that the Ottoman territory between the Tigris and Euphrates rivers was likely to be a good source of high quality (easy to refine) petroleum. But after Pennsylvania, the next major source of petroleum discovered was near the town of Baku, in Azerbaijan, where Robert Nobel (older brother of Alfred) started developing an oil industry. That was in 1873. By the end of the century, the Rothschilds had joined the Nobels in Azerbaijan, still an Ottoman province. By 1900 it was the primary oil producer in the world, albeit landlocked and increasingly dominated by neighboring Czarist Russia.

One of the characteristics of oil in its early exploration and production has been the requirement of large capital investments for exploratory activity associated with unexplored fields surrounding new oil reserves, and costly development expenditures that are subsequently needed for extension and expanding of such fields once they were explored. Therefore, the evolution of the oil industry had not been and cannot be treated in a manner of a mom-and-pop enterprise in which capital has yet to turn into a well-developed process of concentration and centralization. On the other hand, in the late nineteenth century, Taylorism was just giving rise to standardization and thus automated assembly line mass production in need of capital on a scale beyond individual wealth. That is why oil was characterized by the assemblage of several financial syndicates for the venture of exploration in both the United States and abroad. And it is the minimum size of capital that in part plays a pivotal role in development of capitalist competition in oil and in other businesses. The genesis of hydrocarbon can be traced to colonial fusion of capitalistically developed and undeveloped parts of the world—a world whose overwhelming majority had not yet lived within capitalism proper.

But it was not until A.D. 1859 that exploration for oil and gas started in earnest, when the first oil well was drilled by Edwin Drake in northwestern Pennsylvania, United States (some quarters claim it started in 1846 in Azerbaijan). Since then, a lot of advancement took place in the field of oil exploration and production (E&P), and there has been a phenomenal growth in petroleum industry, making it one of the most important sectors in the world influencing global economy and life of the people across the planet.

preface --- 3

introduction --- 9

❖ **Finding Oil and Gas:** ------------------------- 26

1. **Exploration Methods and Techniques** --- 34

   1.1. Geologic Survey --------------------------- 50

   1.2. Geophysical Surveys --------------------- 51

   1.3. Gravity surveys ---------------------------- 53

   1.4. Magnetic surveys ------------------------- 57

   1.5. ELECTRICAL METHODS ------------------ 62

   1.6. RADIOACTIVE METHODS -------------- 64

   1.7. CSEM seabed logging ------------------- 65

   1.8. REMOTE SENSING METHOD ---------- 67

   1.9. GEOCHEMICAL METHODS ------------ 68

   1.10. STRATIGRAPHY ------------------------ 68

   1.11. LIBS Technique for Identification of Crude Oils --- 69

   1.12. SEISMIC SURVEY ---------------------- 72

     1.12.1. THE SEISMIC DETECTIVES ------- 87

     1.12.2. 3D SEISMIC -------------------------- 89

     1.12.3. 4D SEISMIC -------------------------- 92

     1.12.4. Seismotectonics and Seismic Structure 96

- 1.12.5. Seismic Noise Measurements 101
- 1.12.6. Seismic, Semblance Cube/Time Slice Generation ------------------------------105
- 1.12.7. Well to Seismic Integration --108
- 1.12.8. Seismic interpretation ---------109
- 1.12.9. Pre-Drill Seismic Processing and Interpretation (Saudi Arabia) -------------114
- 1.12.10. Fault Interpretation ---------121
- 1.12.11. Horizon Interpretation -----122
- 1.12.12. Possibility to Trigger Seismic Activities on shale gas ----------------------123
2. Exploratory Drilling --------------------------124
3. Development of Oil and Gas Fields -----126
4. Costs and planning--------------------------135
   - 4.1. Investment in exploration ----------136
   - 4.2. Oil Sand Exploration ------------------165
   - 4.3. Existing Research on Gas Hydrates 166
   - 4.4. Hydrocarbon Leads and Implication for Exploration and Production -------------171
   - 4.5. Oil Mining -----------------------------173
   - 4.6. Tar Sand Mining-----------------------174
   - 4.7. Non-mining Methods-----------------175

5. Land and leasing----------------------------180
    5.1. Petroleum Agreements and Bidding 185
    5.2. The Invitation to Bid------------------186
    5.3. The Oil Rent and General Equilibrium 195
    5.4. Theory of Oil Rent and Ownership of the Oil Reserves --------------------------------202
    5.5. The Regime of the 50–50 Profit-Sharing --211
    5.6. Contractual regimes: basic characteristics-----------------------------------214
    5.7. Production sharing contract--------217
    5.8. Risk service contracts-----------------222
    5.9. Risk sharing ----------------------------223
6. Arctic exploration----------------------------229
    6.1. Basin Analysis -----------------------------229
    6.2. Potential Reservoir Localization-------232
    6.3. Deposit Characterization and Valuation ---233
7. Exploration and Development -----------239
References--250

introduction

Rifted continental margins form in response to continental breakup and the creation of new ocean basins. Heating and thinning of the continental lithosphere at the time of rifting causes a localized subsidence and the accumulation of synrift sediments. Towards the ending of rifting, the heated and thinned margin cools and post-rift sediments accumulate.

The emplacement of large, loads on a rifted margin has major implications for its thermal and mechanical evolution.

This is particularly well seen at margins that have been subject to large orogenic loads. For example, the emplacement of Semail Ophiolite in the northern Oman mountains onto the Arabian rifted margin moved the post-rift sedimentary sequences (e.g., Upper Jurassic source rocks) from relatively shallow to deep depths and into the oil window in response of formation of a foreland basin.

Foreland basins develop by lithospheric flexure in front of migrating thrust and fold loads. They are usually "wedge-shaped" in cross-section and are infilled by sediments that have mainly been derived from the adjacent thrust and fold belt. The foreland basin is separated from the orogenic belt by a major advancing thrust front and from the cratonic interior by a peripheral bulge. There is evidence that the bulge may migrate across a foreland basin, both towards and away from the thrust and fold belt, and that they may, in some cases, act as a localized sediment source. For example, Patton and O'Connor suggest that in the case of the northern Oman foreland basin that the flexural bulge migrated across the foredeep towards the craton.

Foreland basins comprise a distinct stratigraphic 'architecture', usually involving onlap as clastic clinoform wedges move out across the basin and then off lap as the depositional Centre migrates in towards the surface and buried loads and the basin fills. Forward modelling studies have shown that the patterns of onlap and off lap are mainly controlled by the rate of migration of the thrust and fold belt, the flexural response of the underlying basement, and the rate of sediment flux into the basin.

The United Arab Emirates (UAE) is underlain by a deep sedimentary basin which comprises a lower rifted passive margin sequence and upper foreland basin (Aruma and Pabdeh) sequences. Previous studies suggest that the UAE foreland basin developed by flexural loading of an underlying rifted continental margin. The rifted margin sequence (that includes Araej, Sila, Thamama and Wasia

Groups) comprise predominantly shelf carbonates with minor deposits of evaporites and clastics that formed during the Late Permian to Late Cretaceous following breakup of the Arabian Plate and Cimmerian Terrane as well as the formation of Tethyan oceanic crust. The lower foreland basin (or Aruma basin) sequence comprises mainly deep-marine mudstones of the Fiqa and Juweiza formations that formed in the Late Cretaceous (Late Coniacian to Campanian) during ophiolite emplacement and thrust and fold loading onto the previously rifted continental margin.

The upper foreland basin (Pabdeh basin) is infilled by shales, marls and limestones that formed as a result of the

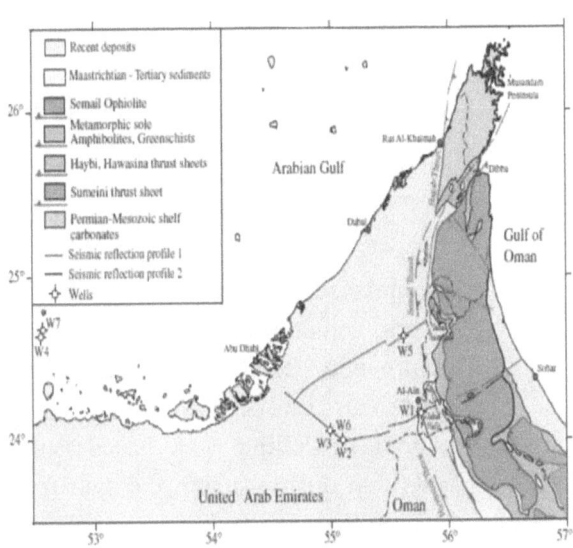

Fig. 6.1 Simplified regional geological map of the United Arab Emirates and northern Oman mountains, modified from Searle (2007). The thick *black* and *blue lines* and *open circles* show the location of the seismic reflection profiles and exploratory wells used in this paper

Mid-Tertiary uplifting and thrust-culminating Musandam shelf carbonates.

Back stripping techniques have proved a powerful technique with which to quantify the tectonic subsidence and uplift of rift-type and foreland basins. However, although there have been a number of stratigraphic studies of the rifted margin sequences that are exposed in the northeastern.

UAE and northern Oman mountains, there have been few quantitative studies of their subsidence and uplift history. As a result, we know little about the thermal and mechanical properties of the Tethyan rifted margin. One problem has been that the exposures are deformed and so it is difficult to restore their thickness. The best record of the subsidence and uplift history, we believe, is in the relatively undeformed rifted margin sequences that underlie the UAE foreland basin.

Recently, Ali and Watts deduced the crustal structure of the northern Oman mountains and UAE foreland basin from the thermal modelling of exploration wells and flexure and gravity modelling of both surface and subsurface (i.e. buried) loads. However, the thermal modelling was based on exploration wells that did not reach the synrift sequence of the Late Permian Tethyan margin. The main aim of this paper is, therefore, to use seismic reflection profiles and deep exploratory wells together with modern basin analysis techniques, to determine the tectonic subsidence and uplift history of the Arabian rifted margin and overlying foreland basins. The basin is of tectonic significance because it formed by ophiolite obduction and Musandam culmination in the northern Oman mountains and flexural loading of the underlying Tethyan rifted margin. [1]

---

[1] Khalid Al Hosani • Francois Roure • Richard Ellison • Stephen Lokier: Lithosphere Dynamics and Sedimentary Basins: The Arabian Plate and Analogues. Springer-Verlag Berlin Heidelberg 2013. P 127: 128

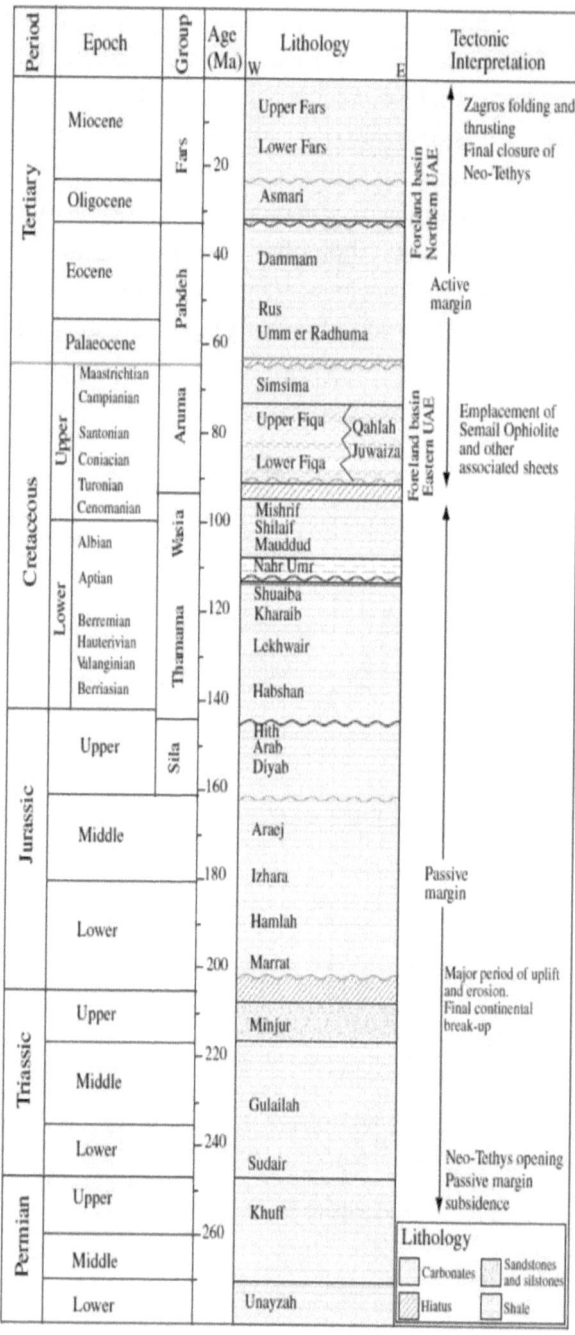

Fig. 6.2 Summary stratigraphic column of the UAE foreland basin. Modified from Ali and Watts (2009)

Petroleum Exploration

Exploration for petroleum originated in the latter part of the nineteenth century when geologists began to map land features that were favorable for the collection of oil in a reservoir. Of particular interest to geologists were outcrops that provided evidence of alternating layers of porous and impermeable rock. The porous rock (typically a sandstone, limestone, or dolomite) provides the reservoir for the petroleum while the impermeable rock (typically clay or shale) prevents migration of the petroleum from the reservoir.

By the early part of the twentieth century, most of the areas where surface structural characteristics offered the promise of oil had been investigated and the era of subsurface exploration for oil began in the early 1920s. New geological and geophysical techniques were developed for areas where the strata were not sufficiently exposed to permit surface mapping of the subsurface characteristics.

In the 1960s, the development of geophysics provided methods for exploring below the surface of the earth.

The principles used are basically magnetism (magnetometer), gravity (gravimeter), and sound waves (seismograph). These techniques are based on the physical properties of materials that can be utilized for measurements and include those that are responsive to the methods of applied geophysics. Furthermore, the methods can be subdivided into those that focus on gravitational properties, magnetic properties, seismic properties, electrical properties, electromagnetic properties, properties, and radioactive properties. These geophysical methods can be subdivided into two principal groups: (1) those methods without depth control and (2) those methods having depth control.

In the first group of the measurements (those without depth control), the methods incorporate effects from both local and distant sources. For example, gravity measurements are affected by the variation in the radius of the earth with latitude.

They are also affected by the elevation of the site relative to sea level, the thickness of the earth's crust, and the configuration and density of the underlying rocks, as well as by any abnormal mass variation that might be associated with a mineral deposit.

In the second group of measurements (those with depth control), seismic or electric energy is introduced into the ground and variations in transmissibility with distance are observed and interpreted in terms of geological quantities. Depths to geological horizons having marked differences in transmissibility can be computed on a quantitative basis and the physical nature of these horizons deduced.

However, geophysical exploration techniques cannot be applied indiscriminately.

Knowledge of the geological parameters likely to be associated with the mineral or subsurface condition being studied is essential both in choosing the method to be applied and in interpreting the results obtained. Furthermore, not all the techniques described here may be suitable for petroleum exploration. In petroleum exploration, terms as geophysical borehole logging can imply the use of one or more of the geophysical exploration techniques. This procedure involves drilling a well and using instruments to log or make measurements at various levels in the hole by such means as gravity (density), electrical resistivity, or radioactivity.

A basic rule of thumb in the upstream (or producing) sector of the oil and gas industry has been (and maybe still is in some circles of exploration technology) that the best place to find new crude oil or natural gas is near formations where it has already been found. The financial risk of doing so is far lower than that associated with drilling a rank wildcat hole in a prospective, but previously unproductive, area.

On the other hand, there is a definite tradeoff between rewards for risk. The returns on drilling investment become ever leaner as more wells are drilled in a particular area because the natural distribution of oil and gas field volumes tends to be approximately log-geometric – there are only a few large fields, whereas there are a great many small ones.

Drilling does not end when production commences and continues after a field enters production. Extension wells must be drilled to define the boundaries of the crude oil pool. In-field wells are necessary to increase recovery rates, and service wells are used to reopen wells that have become clogged. Additionally, wells are often drilled at the same location but to different depths, to test other geological structures for the presence of crude oil.

Finally, the drilling job is complete when the drill bit penetrates the reservoir and the reservoir is evaluated to see whether the well represents the discovery of a prospect or whether it is a dry hole. If the hole is dry, it is plugged and abandoned.

At the stage when the prospect has been identified, reservoir evaluation is usually initiated by examining the cuttings from the well bore for evidence of hydrocarbons while the drill bit passes through a reservoir trap. The evaluation of these cuttings helps pinpoint the possible producing intervals in the well bore.

At this time, a wire-line is lowered into the hole and an electric log is run to help define possible producing intervals, presence of hydrocarbons, and detailed information about the different formations throughout the well bore. Further tests (such as pressure tests, formation fluid recovery, and sidewall core analysis) can also be run on individual formations within the well bore.

If hydrocarbons are detected, the prospect becomes a live prospect and once the final depth has been reached, the well is completed to allow oil to flow into the casing in a controlled manner. First, a perforating gun is lowered into the well to the production depth. The gun has explosive charges to create holes in the casing through which oil can flow. After the casing has been perforated, a small-diameter pipe (tubing) is run into the hole as a conduit for oil and gas to flow up the well and a packer is run down the outside of the tubing. When the packer is set at the production level, it is expanded to form a seal around the outside of the tubing.

Finally, a multivalve structure is installed at the top of the tubing and cemented to the top of the casing. The Christmas tree allows them to control the flow of oil from the well.

Finally, the development of an onshore shallow gas reservoir located among other established fields may be expected to incur relatively high cost and be nominally complex. A deep oil or gas reservoir located in more than 1 mile of water depth located miles away from other existing producing fields will push the limits of emerging technology at extreme costs.

Onshore developments may permit the phasing of facility investments as wells are drilled and production established to minimize economic risk. However, offshore projects may require 65%or more of the total planned investments to be made before production start-up and impose significant economic risk.

As might be expected, the type of exploration technique employed depends upon the nature of the site. In other words, and as for many environmental operations, the recovery techniques applied to a specific site are dictated by the nature of the site and are, in fact, site specific. For example, in areas where little is known about the subsurface, preliminary reconnaissance techniques are necessary to identify potential reservoir systems that warrant further investigation. Techniques for reconnaissance that have been employed to make inferences about the subsurface structure include satellite and high-altitude imagery and magnetic and gravity surveys. [1]

Petroleum Exploration

At the end of the twentieth century, two technological innovations were developed that greatly increased the volume of economically recoverable oil reserves in North America. The first of these, hydraulic fracturing, or fracking, was originally developed to enhance the production of natural gas. But over the next 5–10 years, this technique was adopted for production of crude oil, leading to substantial increases in production. At about the same time, developments in the use of sophisticated imaging, such as 3-D imaging, increased the accuracy of exploratory ventures.

Together, these techniques made exploration and development of new deposits more efficient and contributed to the rapid increase in US oil and gas production that has occurred in the past 10 years or so. These efforts led to the development of new hydrocarbon sources from formations that had previously been regarded as uneconomic, particularly shale oil formations in Texas and North Dakota, and offshore resources located in the deep waters of the Gulf of Mexico. Both new sources of oil turned out to be quite prolific. [1]

---

[1] Ripudaman Malhotra: Fossil Energy. Springer Science+Business Media New York 2013. P 27: 30
[1] Congrui Jin • Gianluca Cusatis: New Frontiers in Oil and Gas Exploration. Springer International Publishing Switzerland 2016. P 507

Exploration for petroleum originated in the latter part of the nineteenth century when geologists began to map land features to search out favorable places to drill for oil. Of particular interest to geologists were outcrops that provided evidence of alternating layers of porous and impermeable rock. The porous rock (typically a sandstone, limestone, or dolomite) provides the reservoir for petroleum; the impermeable rock (typically clay or shale) acts as a trap and prevents migration of the petroleum from the reservoir.

By the early twentieth century, most of the areas where surface structural characteristics offered the promise of oil had been investigated and the era of subsurface exploration for oil began in the early 1920s. New geological and geophysical techniques were developed for areas where the strata were not sufficiently exposed to permit surface mapping of the subsurface characteristics. In the 1960s, the development of geophysics provided methods for exploring below the surface of the earth.

The principles used are basically magnetism (magnetometer), gravity (gravimeter), and sound waves (seismograph). These techniques are based on the physical properties of materials that can be utilized for measurements and include those that are responsive to the methods of applied geophysics.

Further, the methods can be subdivided into those that focus on gravitational properties, magnetic properties, seismic properties, electrical properties, electromagnetic properties, and radioactive properties. These geophysical methods can be subdivided into the following two groups: (1) those without depth control and (2) those with depth control.

In the first group, the measurements incorporate spontaneous effects from both local and distant sources over which the observer has no control. For example, gravity measurements are affected by the variation in the radius of the earth with latitude. They are also affected by the elevation of the site relative to sea level, the thickness of the earth's crust, and the configuration and density of the underlying rocks, as well as by any abnormal mass variation that might be associated with a mineral deposit. In the last stages of assessment, the interpretation always depends upon the geological knowledge of the interpreter.

In the second group of measurements (those with depth control), seismic or electric energy is introduced into the ground and variations in transmissibility with distance are observed and interpreted in terms of geological quantities. Thus, depths to geological horizons with marked differences in transmissibility can be computed on a quantitative basis and the physical nature of these horizons deduced. The accuracy, ease of interpretation, and applicability of all methods falling into this group are not the same, and there are natural and economic conditions under which the measurements of the first group are preferable for exploration studies despite their inherent limitations.

However, it must be recognized that geophysical exploration techniques cannot be applied indiscriminately. Knowledge of the geological parameters likely to be associated with the mineral or subsurface condition being studied is essential, both in choosing the method to be applied and in interpreting the results obtained. Further, not all the techniques described here may be suitable for petroleum exploration. Nevertheless, the techniques that are described here are included as it is valuable to know their nature and how they might be applied to subsurface exploration.

It should also be noted that such terms as geophysical borehole logging can imply the use of one or more of the geophysical exploration techniques. This procedure involves drilling a well and using instruments to log or make measurements at various levels in the hole by such means as gravity (density), electrical resistivity, or radioactivity. In addition, formation samples (cores) are taken for physical and chemical tests. [1]

---

[1]James G. Speight: The Chemistry and Technology of Petroleum. FOURTH EDITION. Taylor & Francis Group, LLC. 2007. P 134:135

❖ Finding Oil and Gas:

oil and gas exist in reservoirs located thousands of feet below the earth's surface and ocean floors. These reservoirs would exist only in certain locations depending on the geologic history of the earth. Therefore, determining the location of petroleum reservoirs is a very difficult task and probably is the most challenging aspect of the petroleum industry. Finding or discovering a petroleum reservoir involves three major activities: geologic surveying, geophysical surveying, and exploratory drilling activities. The following sections provide a brief background on each of these activities. [1]

The first concept of oil reserves closely embraced the amounts of oil available in tapped reservoirs. Forecasting techniques like the volumetric and historical–statistical methods required that some successful drilling had already been carried out. In this sense, reserves resulted in ex-post measurements, with geologists tracking a path previously opened by wildcatters and oil companies. Considering the epochal criteria, two omissions stand out as particularly relevant:

---

[1] Hussein K. Abdel-Aal Mohamed A. Aggour Mohamed A. Fahim: Petroleum and Gas Field Processing. Second Edition. Taylor & Francis Group, LLC. 2016. P 6

- The first is the failure to account for enhanced recovery practices implemented in pools that had long since passed their maturity, such as New York and Pennsylvania. In these regions, continued production was maintained chiefly by cleaning and deepening old wells or by obtaining oil from shallow sands, which had been thought too insignificant when the wells were first drilled. Thanks to these recovery methods, new oil from exhausted fields could be added to the reserves existing. While only small amounts were at stake in the 1910s, the importance of enhanced recovery methods (ERH) would attain new heights in the 1920s with the injection of gas, the injection of compressed air and flooding water into reservoirs on the verge of exhaustion. Fostered by a string of technological improvements, recovery techniques rebounded again in the 1950s and 1960s with steam injection, the injection of water solutions with polymers, surfactants, or caustic chemicals, in situ combustion, and electric hydraulic shocks.

- The second was the omission of prospective and untapped reserves. To put the 1909 oil survey into perspective, it is worth recalling that for nearly 50 years geological coal surveys had followed the practice of ascertaining the recoverable coal left behind in pits plus assessment of seams with "hidden coal." Referred to as existent, probable and possible reserves, this assessment was quantitative in nature. Insofar as oil reserves were equated as fixed assets, the depletion of reservoirs could somehow be thought of as the depletion of a non-renewable forest. The geological survey thus became a contentious issue that carved a trench between the business view of a drifting amount determined by new discoveries and the official view of a fixed amount determined by the already confirmed oil reservoirs. Hence, the stage was set for a public confrontation between those who claimed "a petroleum famine is imminent" and those who countervailed with "there will always be enough petroleum to meet demand.

Henceforth, surveys were clouded by the suspicion that the conservative nature of the forecasts set the tone for those who argued in favor of government interference through regulation, prorationing, production controls, waste disposal, or even— the rumors persisted— partial nationalization. In an attempt to calm these troubled waters, in 1922 the USGS mobilized 10 geologists representing the American Association of Petroleum Geologists and six from the USGS for a comprehensive and accurate study aimed at once and for all stemming the controversies and bringing the debate back to indisputably geological grounds. For the first time, the distinction between known fields and undiscovered reservoirs was acknowledged. The oilman's view of exhaustion discovery cycles was translated into probabilistic categorizations that accounted for "prospective" and "possible" oil. The concluding estimate identified 5 billion (5×10^9) barrels of crude "in sight" and an additional 4 billion barrels as "prospective" and "possible." The former was judged "reasonably reliable" with the latter deemed absolutely "speculative and hazardous." In the end, neither the enhanced accuracy of petroleum in sight nor the acknowledgment of "speculative" discoveries reassured the industry. On the contrary, the enduring politicization of the geological survey opened the door to the institutionalization of competing reports on petroleum reserves sponsored by the government, by specialized reviews, and by the American Petroleum Institute business association. From 1922 onwards, this pluralism of estimates became the rule: each vested interest, each major institution produced its own forecasts. Maybe the surprising issue in this evolution toward customized surveys is that there were hardly any discrepancies in the final figures of proven reserves, although that did not halt public and private bickering between institutions.

The crux of the matter was naturally the amount of oil still undiscovered. In this regard, the uncertainty could hardly be solved. There were bold stands on the subject, but little means to figure out a reasonable and acceptable forecast.

As regards finding oil, geological knowledge had limited utility: It could forecast where oil was not supposed to be found (for instance in rocks dating from the Jurassic, Permian, and Silurian Eras), and it could provide some advice on defining areas worth exploring (areas of extensive limestone dolomitization, salt domes, or beds of porous sandstone lying within shales). Nevertheless, the only way to be certain about oil reserves was to drill; as an experienced field-worker reported: "geologists have gone deeply into the matter and in a way seem to be able to select oil producing territory. But they are not infallible. A hole in the ground seems to be the only sure test. [1]

A final piece in this puzzle may be called luck, coincidence, or the unexpected coincidence of different series of events: In 1926 and 1927, a series of discoveries in Oklahoma, Texas, and New Mexico hit some of the largest oil concentrations in the world, adding almost five thousand million (5×10^9) barrels overnight to the proven reserves of the USA. The frenzied oil boom that ensued flooded the markets and drove prices down, silencing the "famine," "shortage," and "exhaustion" theses for the next

[1] Nuno Luis Madureira: Key Concepts in Energy. Springer International Publishing Switzerland 2014. P 112: 114

50 years. Institutions that had been founded to deal with scarcity and to fight "waste" were subsequently reshuffled to enforce conservation through the self-regulation of the industry. Overall, the rise of geophysical exploration played a minor role in this spurt (circumscribed to part of East Texas) as most of the discoveries resulted from wildcat drilling practices and surface indicator insights. Hence, the urgency that had once turned geophysical exploration into a key science for the future of humanity became less momentous. Conservationist ideas were also hit. The oil being endlessly pumped out of the earth simply washed away the bleak predictions of the early 1910s.

The history of estimating oil reserves proved to be a history of long-lasting misunderstandings. Although American geologists combined volumetric and statistical methods specifically tailored to the realities of the petroleum industry, the final figures from the first oil survey, released in 1909, came to be interpreted by analogy with the forest conservation practices and policies. The discovery of 15 billion barrels of oil left in reservoirs was regarded as a sort of opening shot in a race against the clock of depletion. "Proven Reserves" were understood as a stock; a finite stock that had to be economized, held back, and set aside for future uses or contingencies. By adopting terminologies with familiar nontechnical meanings, and furthermore colored by the moving debate on presidential powers and federal forest "reserves," geologists ascribed the meaning of the concept to an observable fixed asset. Furthermore, given there was, after all, not so much of it left underground, they conveyed the idea that America was approaching its resource supply potential. What ensued was a sort of pathological split between the "scarcity" and the "overflowing" stances, a split sturdily entrenched in discourses, social networks, newspapers, journals, and institutions.

To counteract looming claims over the need for regulation, the API—American Petroleum Institute set up its own survey, based on preferential access to oilfields and business records, thereby building a spotless reputation for data gathering. Its aim was to replace geological uncertainties by a narrow but accurate appraisal of oil reserves. Between 1925 and 1935, all open possibilities were locked-into the concept of "proven reserves," grounded on technical and economic feasibility.

Such closure ran against the grain of current technological improvements as it excluded probabilistic methods of oil finding by the geophysical sciences and neglected the still novel enhanced oil-recovery practices. This means that, in the end, economic–political factors superseded the evolution in technology and science. [1]

---

[1] Nuno Luis Madureira: Key Concepts in Energy. Springer International Publishing Switzerland 2014. P 118: 119

1. Exploration Methods and Techniques

The selection of a drilling site is a tricky and costly affair. Though some visible evidence of a hydrocarbon source, like seepage of oil and gas from the surface, the visual appearance of surface and vegetation, the presence of oil or gas in fountains or rivers, etc., are sometimes used in locating oil and gas reserves, and many ancient oil fields were discovered by these events. But, today, such fortunate events are very rare and sometimes may not always be suitable for commercial exploitation.

Modern exploration techniques use geophysical, geochemical, and geotechnical methods. Exploration of the surface of Earth can be useful for imaging or mapping sub-surface structures favorable for oil and gas accumulation. In the geophysical methods, gravimetric, magneto metric, seismic, radioactive, and stratigraphic studies of the surface are gathered. Chemical analysis of the surface soil and rocks are carried out by geochemical methods. Geotechnical methods, such as the mechanical properties of rocks and surface, are measured. Remote sensing from satellite is the most recent development for a low cost geological survey. Usual geophysical methods include gravimetric, magneto metric, and seismic methods. Geochemical methods employ chemical analysis of the cuttings (rock samples cut by drilling bit) and core (a narrow column of rock taken from the wall of a drilled hole) of the drilled site. [1]

The objective of any exploration venture is to find new volumes of hydrocarbons at a low cost and in a short period of time. Exploration budgets are in direct competition with acquisition opportunities. If a company spends more money finding oil than it would do to buy the equivalent amount 'in the market place' there is little incentive to continue exploration. Conversely, a company which manages to find new reserves at low cost has a significant competitive edge since it can afford more exploration, find and develop reservoirs more profitably and can target and develop smaller prospects.

Once an area has been selected for exploration, the usual sequence of technical activities starts with the definition of a basin. The mapping of gravity anomalies and magnetic anomalies will be the first two methods applied. In many cases this data will be available in the public domain or can be bought as a 'non-exclusive' survey.

---

[1]Uttam Ray Chaudhuri: Fundamentals of Petroleum and Petrochemical Engineering. Taylor and Francis Group. 2011. P 9

Next, a coarse two-dimensional (2D) seismic grid, covering a wide area, will be acquired in order to define leads, areas which show for instance a structure which potentially contains an accumulation. Recently electro-magnetic techniques have also been deployed at this stage to assist in the delineation of basins and the identification of potential hydrocarbon accumulations. A particular exploration concept, often the idea of an individual or a team will emerge next. Since at this point very few hard facts are available to judge the merit of these ideas they are often referred to as 'play'.

More detailed investigations will be integrated to define a 'prospect', a subsurface structure with a reasonable probability of containing all the elements of a petroleum accumulation, namely source rock, maturation, migration, reservoir rock and trap. [1]

Finding a petroleum reservoir may at first seem to be like finding a needle in a haystack. Given the cost of exploration ventures, it is clear that much effort will be expended to avoid failures. A variety of disciplines are involved, such as geology, geophysics, mathematics, geochemistry, to analyze a prospective area. However, on average, even in

---

[1] Frank Jahn, Mark Cook and Mark Graham: HYDROCARBON EXPLORATION AND PRODUCTION. 2ND EDITION. Elsevier B.V. 2008. P 24

very mature areas where exploration has been ongoing for years, only every third exploration well will encounter substantial amounts of hydrocarbons.

In basins that have not been drilled before the rate of success may be as low as every tenth well. The first indication that an area is a potential candidate for closer geophysical exploration, is the general knowledge the geologists have of the area.

Mapping of gravity anomalies and magnetic anomalies may be the first indications of a sedimentary basin. Next, seismic surveying is carried out, starting with a coarse two-dimensional (2D) seismic grid, covering a wide area. This is performed to find structures that may be candidates for potential hydrocarbon accumulations. These seismic surveying methods, which are described in more detail below, are based on sending acoustic pulses into the strata and recording the reflections. Recently, also electromagnetic techniques using electromagnetic pulses have been used.

Acoustic seismic surveys involve generating sound waves which propagate through the Earth's rock down to reservoir targets. For land surveys this may be truck-mounted vibrating sources or small dynamite charges detonated in a shallow hole. The most common marine sources are pneumatic air guns or water guns that expel air or water into the surrounding water column to create an acoustic pulse. The waves are reflected from different strata in the underground and registered on the surface in receivers called hydrophones. The reflection data is recorded and stored for processing. The result is an acoustic image of the subsurface which is interpreted by geophysicists and geologists. It is quite clear that this involves a complicated analysis that need highly trained and experienced specialists. Their work is decisive for where the first wells will be drilled.

Seismic surveying has progressed to become one of the most effective methods for optimizing field production. It is used in:

• exploration for delineating structural and stratigraphic traps

• deciding where the first wells will be drilled

• field appraisal and development for estimating reserves, and drawing up field development plans

• production for reservoir surveillance such as observing the movement of reservoir fluids in response to production

Seismic acquisition techniques vary depending on the environment (onshore or offshore) and the purpose of the survey. In an exploration phase a seismic survey consist of a loose grid of 2D lines. In contrast, in an underground appraisal, a 3D seismic survey will be shot. The 3D grid is more closely spaced than the 2D and have both vertical and horizontal positions. In some mature fields a permanent 3D acquisition network might be installed on the seabed for regular (6–12 months) surveillance of the reservoir's response to production. A collection of three-dimensional (3D) seismic data acquired at different times over the same area is called a four-dimensional (4D) seismic acquisition. [1]

Seismic data acquisition and geological models give important information about the size and the commercial capacity of a reservoir. However, it does not inform us about the flow properties of the reservoir fluids and their interaction with the rock.

These fluids (water, oil, gas) are contained under high pressure in a porous network with pore sizes ranging from a few μm (10^{-6} m) to several hundred μm. Once the reservoir is opened to the surface through a production well, the high pressure in the reservoir will drive the hydrocarbon towards the well and produce it to the surface. Utilizing the

---

[1]Patrick A. Narbel • Jan Petter Hansen Jan R. Lien: Energy Technologies and Economics. Springer International Publishing Switzerland 2014. P 74: 75

natural pressure of the reservoir called *pressure depletion*, is the simplest of all production mechanisms. The following expansion of the reservoir fluids act as a source of drive energy which support the *primary production* from the reservoir. Primary production means using the natural energy stored in the reservoir as a drive mechanism for production. *Secondary production* implies adding energy to the reservoir by injecting fluids to help supporting the reservoir pressure as production takes place. One also speaks of *tertiary recovery* or *enhanced oil recovery* (EOR) which implies adding energy through thermal methods, chemical flooding or injection of gas, for example CO_2 or nitrogen. [1]

Geophysical methods for exploring for hydrocarbons are usually subdivided into potential methods and seismic methods. Potential methods measure variations in the gravity and magnetic fields and predict the gross geologic features of a basin. Seismic methods provide detailed information on the structure and stratigraphic features of the sedimentary layers and in some cases can locate hydrocarbons directly.

---

[1] Patrick A. Narbel • Jan Petter Hansen Jan R. Lien: Energy Technologies and Economics. Springer International Publishing Switzerland 2014. P 79: 80

Magnetic measurements are usually made with an airborne magnetometer, which gives rapid coverage of large areas and provides information on the major features of the igneous basement underlying the sedimentary rocks in the basins. Estimates of depth to basement are the primary quantitative measurements obtained from magnetic surveys; thus, the gross features of the basin framework are established. Ground magnetic measurements provide detail on igneous intrusive that may trap hydrocarbons. [1]

Gravity measurements are usually made at ground stations and provide information about the gross features of the sedimentary section. These measures are very effective in delineating salt structures. In the early days of salt dome exploration, after Spindletop, gravity measurements successfully pinpointed domes and led to the discovery of a number of fields. Even now gravity contour maps are effective in locating deep-seated salt structures that often are reflected into the overlying sedimentary layers and help to isolate areas over which to conduct reflection seismic surveys. Because seismic surveys are very expensive compared to gravity methods, it makes economic sense to isolate areas of potential hydrocarbon accumulation.

---

[1] R.L.Sengbush: petroleum exploration, a quantitative introduction, library of congress 1st edition 1986. p 55

Gravity measurements are made routinely at sea during the course of making seismic surveys, since they add only small increment to the survey cost and provide valuable information about salt and other stratigraphic features. Airborne gravity methods are also used for rapid reconnaissance and gross measurements of the gravitational field. Gravity measurements from a moving platform are affected by the erratic motions of the platform, and the two effects are separated by special filtering techniques that preserve the gravity and filter out the effects due to motion of the platform. [1] 56

Gravity and magnetics are potential methods; that is, they are passive. They depend on measurement of the natural magnetic and gravity fields of the earth. They are ambiguous in that an anomaly with a potential method may arise from a variety of bodies at a variety of depths in the earth. Because the potential methods are ambiguous, quantitative measurements of the nature of the body causing the anomaly must come from outside information. Such information can come from drilling contacts, seismic results, or reasonable geologic limitations. In spite of such ambiguities

---

[1]R.L.Sengbush: petroleum exploration, a quantitative introduction, library of congress 1st edition 1986. P 55: 56

and lack of precision, magnetic and gravity measures can impose very definite limits on geologic interpretations and can thereby make specific and useful contributions to the overall exploration picture.

Seismic methods provide detailed information on structural and stratigraphic features and in some cases, fluid content, by use of refractions and reflections. The earliest seismic measurements used first arrivals that travel the least-time refraction path from source to receiver to gain knowledge of the near surface layers. As the source-to-receiver distance increases, the first arrivals dig deeper and deeper into the earth, giving information on successively deeper layers. The reflection method is now the most widely used geophysical method and operates on the principle of recording back-scattered energy from targets as do radar and sonar. The targets in the reflection method are changes in the acoustic impedance of the subsurface, which give structural, stratigraphic, and hydrocarbon information about the subsurface. [1]

The seismic method is much more direct in its relation to geology than are the potential methods because one can map

---

[1] R.L.Sengbush: petroleum exploration, a quantitative introduction, library of congress 1st edition 1986. P 56

reflections and directly correlate the reflections with geologic strata, giving a relatively accurate measure of their depth and possibly even their stratigraphy. In some cases, however, correlation with geology may be uncertain or misleading, and in such cases, gravity and magnetics may contribute by establishing bounds on possible correlations and provide lithological information.

The seismic method is by far the most widely used geophysical method for hydrocarbon exploration, and it is also the most expensive. Expenditures for the seismic method and its associated data processing account for 95% or more of the total expenditures for petroleum exploration geophysics, and gravity and magnetics are relegated to the remaining 5% or less. As a rough rule of thumb, the relative costs per unit area of magnetic, gravity, and seismic methods stand in the ratio of 1 to 10 to 100. [1]

The presence of pre-existing faults and fractures in the upper crust contribute to induced seismicity as a result of fluid injection, in hydraulic fracturing, deep storage of CO_2, and stimulation of EGS reservoirs. In all of these, either maintaining the low permeability and

---

[1]R.L.Sengbush: petroleum exploration, a quantitative introduction, library of congress 1st edition 1986. p 56

integrity of caprocks or in controlling the growth of permeability in initially very-low-permeability shales and geothermal reservoirs are key desires. Hence, it is of particular interest to understand the seismicity-permeability interaction in caprocks and unconventional reservoirs.

Mechanically, the occurrence of induced seismicity depends on the shear strength and the frictional stability of a fault-which in-turn depends on its mineralogical composition. The weakness of natural faults can be explained by the presence of frictionally weak minerals, including talc. Early experiments using synthetic mixtures of salts and muscovite/kaolinite showed that weakening can occur with as low as 10 wt% (weight percentage) of frictionally weak minerals. Shear experiments using mixtures of talc and quartz sand suggested that 30–50 wt% of frictionally weak minerals were required to weaken the composite gouge—much larger percentages than that observed in some natural weak faults. This difference can be explained by the presence of a structured through-going layer of weak minerals (e.g. talc), which weakens the fault. These observations pose the question of what proportion of frictionally weak minerals are needed, and how thick such a layer need be. Experiments suggest that the frictional strength of gouge decreases systematically with an increase in thickness of the talc layer.

Additionally, coupled shear-permeability experiments suggest that the permeability evolution of faults is likely linked to such mineralogical properties.

Permeability is known to change during shear deformation. It has been widely observed that failure may occur stably (aseismically) at slow creep rates of long duration (order of 1–100 mm/year) or unstably (seismically) at fast frictional sliding rates of short duration (order of 1 m/s). The stability of sliding is governed by the frictional properties of faults and can be described with rate-and-state friction laws. These studies provide potential insights into the rheological response of caprocks and unconventional reservoirs with regard to the mode and timing of induced earthquakes. However, it is still unclear whether different styles of permeability evolve from unstable fast sliding of seismic events versus slow-slip aseismic events. In this study, we integrate both experimental and computational methods to (1) explore how fracture permeability changes in response to fracture reactivation; (2) identify hydraulic behavior for different rock types; and (3) probe the relationship between frictional strength with respect to mineralogical composition. [1]

---

[1] Y. Fang . C. Wang . D. Elsworth . T. Ishibashi: Seismicity-permeability coupling in the behavior of gas shales, CO_2 storage and deep geothermal energy. Springer

In the foregoing it is noted that the friction-permeability relationships are complex and challenging. Thus, we first review assumptions that relax the constraints of real systems and to capture the most fundamental features that reveal the permeability evolution during both aseismic and seismic events via experiments. Then, we will introduce the sample materials, preparation processes and experimental setup and procedures. [1]

There are various geophysical surveying methods that are routinely applied in the search for potential hydrocarbon accumulations. Geophysical methods respond to variations in physical properties of the earth's subsurface including its rocks, fluids and voids. They locate boundaries across which changes in properties occur. These changes give rise to an anomaly relative to a background value; this anomaly is the target which the methods are trying to detect.

The measurement of changes in signal strength along lines of a grid or network, 'profiling', allows anomalies to be mapped out spatially. Care should be taken to avoid spatial 'aliasing', the loss of fine detail information as a

---

International Publishing Switzerland 2017. P 1: 2
([1])Y. Fang . C. Wang . D. Elsworth . T. Ishibashi: Seismicity-permeability coupling in the behavior of gas shales, CO_2 storage and deep geothermal energy. Springer International Publishing Switzerland 2017. P 2

result of gathering data at only a small number of measuring stations. Time and budget often come into play at this stage.

It is important to remember that the mere acquisition and processing of data do not guarantee success of a survey: information is not equal to knowledge.

Interpretation of geophysical data should always be carried out within a sound geological framework. Often several methods are used to complement one another or they are used in conjunction with other disciplines to develop a geologically

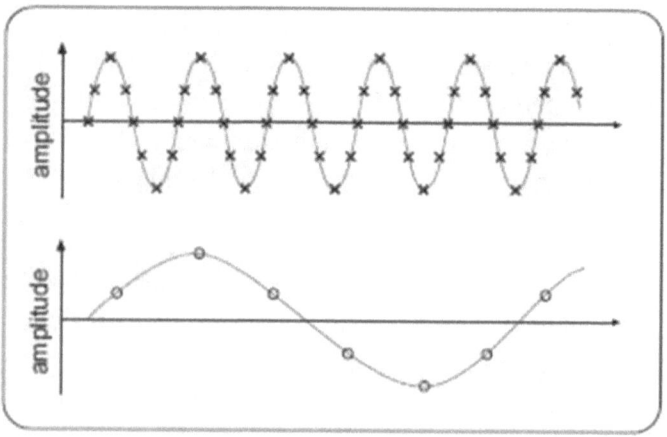

If the sample frequency is high e.g. measuring at times marked by a cross, then the wave is sampled adequantely with faithful representation of the input data.

Petroleum Exploration

If the sample frequency is low e.g. measuring at times marked by a circle, then the wave is sampled inadequantely with loss of the high frequency information and distortion of the input data.

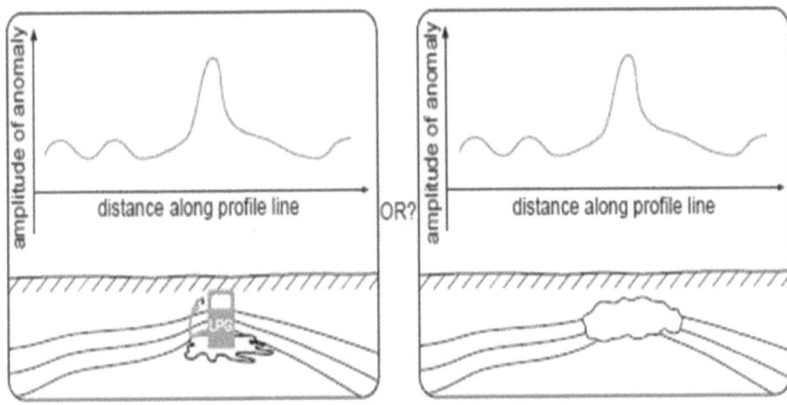

meaningful model that can explain the observed anomalies. This helps to reduce uncertainties and to address the principle of equivalence or 'non-uniqueness' where one anomaly can be modelled in a variety of ways. [1]

1.1. Geologic Survey

Geologic surveying is the oldest and first used tool for determining potential locations of underground petroleum reservoirs. It involves examination of the surface geology, formation

---

[1] Frank Jahn, Mark Cook and Mark Graham: HYDROCARBON EXPLORATION AND PRODUCTION. 2ND EDITION. Elsevier B.V. 2008. P 25: 26

outcrops, and surface rock samples. The collected information is used in conjunction with geologic theories to determine whether petroleum reservoirs could be present underground at the surveyed location. The results of the geologic survey are not conclusive and only offer a possibility of finding petroleum reservoirs. The rate of success of finding petroleum reservoirs using geologic surveys alone has been historically low. Currently, geologic surveys are used together with other geophysical surveys to provide higher rates of success in finding petroleum reservoirs. [1]

1.2. Geophysical Surveys

There are mainly four types of geophysical surveys used in the industry: gravity survey, magnetic survey, seismic survey, and remote sensing.

The gravity survey is the least expensive method of locating a possible petroleum reservoir. It involves the use of an instrument, a gravimeter, which picks up a reflection of the density of the subsurface rock. For example, because salt is less dense than rocks, the gravimeter can detect the presence of salt domes, which would indicate the presence of an anticline structure. Such a structure is a

---

[1]Hussein K. Abdel-Aal Mohamed A. Aggour Mohamed A. Fahim: Petroleum and Gas Field Processing. Second Edition. Taylor & Francis Group, LLC. 2016. P 7

candidate for possible accumulation of oil and gas.

The magnetic survey involves measurement of the magnetic pull, which is affected by the type and depth of the subsurface rocks. The magnetic survey can be used to determine the existence and depth of subsurface volcanic formations, or basement rocks, which contain high concentrations of magnetite. Such information is utilized to identify the presence of sedimentary formations above the basement rocks.

The seismic survey involves sending strong pressure (sound) waves through the earth and receiving the reflected waves off the various surfaces of the subsurface rock layers. The sound waves are generated either by using huge land vibrators or using explosives. The very large amount of data collected, which include the waves' travel times and characteristics, are analyzed to provide definitions of the subsurface geological structures and to determine the locations of traps that are suitable for petroleum accumulation.

This type of survey is the most important and most accurate of all of the geophysical surveys. Significant technological developments in the field of seismic surveying have been achieved in recent years. Improvements in the data collection, manipulation, analysis, and interpretation have increased the significance and accuracy of seismic surveying. Further, the development of three-dimensional (3D) seismic surveying technology has made it possible to provide 3D descriptions of the subsurface geologic structures.

Remote sensing is a modern technique that involves using infrared, heat-sensitive color photography to detect the presence of underground mineral deposits, water, faults, and other structural features. The sensing device, normally on a satellite, feeds the signals into special computers that produces maps of the subsurface structures. [1]

1.3. Gravity surveys

The gravity method measures small variations of the earth's gravity field caused by density variations in geological structures. The measuring tool is a sophisticated form of spring balance designed to be responsive over a wide range of values.

Fluctuations in the gravity field give rise to changes in the spring length which are measured (relative to a base station value) at various stations along the profile of a 2D

---

[1]Hussein K. Abdel-Aal Mohamed A. Aggour Mohamed A. Fahim: Petroleum and Gas Field Processing. Second Edition. Taylor & Francis Group, LLC. 2016. P 7: 8

network. The measurements are corrected for latitudinal position and elevation of the recording station to define the 'Bouguer' anomaly.

The development of airborne gravity technology has allowed the surveying of previously inaccessible areas and of much larger basins than is currently practical with land-based measuring tools. [1]

Gravity methods are based on the measurement of physical quantities related to the gravitational field, which in turn are affected by differences in the density and the disposition of underlying geological bodies. In oil and gas exploration, in which no direct density control is associated with the material being sought, exploration is based on the mapping of geological structures to determine situations that might localize the material being sought. In such cases, the significant density values are salt 2.1 to 2.2, igneous rocks 2.5 to 3.0, and sedimentary rocks 1.6 to 2.8. The last value increases with depth owing to consolidation and geological age, and as a result, structural deformation associated with faults and folding can be detected. Compaction of sediments over edges or knolls on the underlying crystalline rock surface also

---

[1]Frank Jahn, Mark Cook and Mark Graham: HYDROCARBON EXPLORATION AND PRODUCTION. 2ND EDITION. Elsevier B.V. 2008. P 26

leads to a local increase in mass, as does the development of calcareous cap rock over the heads of intrusive salt columns.

Thus, the gravimeter detects differences in gravity and gives an indication of the location and density of underground rock formations. Differences from the normal can be caused by geological and other influences, and such differences provide an indication of subsurface structural formations. In the early days of gravity prospecting, both the torsion balance and the pendulum apparatus were extensively employed, but these have been supplanted by spring balance systems (gravimeters). The latter can be read in a matter of minutes, in contrast to the several hours required in obtaining readings with the earlier instruments.

There is a variety of gravimeters, but those in common use consist essentially of a weighted boom that pivots about a hinge point. The boom is linked to a spring system so that the unit is essentially unstable and hence very sensitive to slight variations in gravitational attraction.

Deflections of the boom from a central (zero) position are measured by observing the change in the tension in the spring system required to bring the boom back to that position. Readings are taken from a graduated dial on the head of the instrument that is attached to the spring system through a screw. There must be an accurate calibration of the screw, reading dial, and spring response for the readings to have gravitational significance.

Gravimeters can also be employed for use in shallow water. Thus, use of watertight housings with automatic leveling and electronic reading devices allows gravimeter surveys to be carried out in aqueous environments. Other gravimeters have been developed for use in submarines and on gyro-stabilized platforms on surface ships as well as in aircraft. [1]

Gravity of the earth's surface varies with distance from the surface of Earth and the type of material, such as salt, water, oil, gas, or mineral matter. The measurement of a small variation of gravity or acceleration due to gravity is recorded with accuracy and the data are converted to retrieve a geological structure of the sub-surface of Earth. A gravimeter is a very sensitive instrument, usually a spring-type balance with high resolution and accuracy capable of detecting a minute variation in gravity.

Porous and oil-containing rock layers and salt have lower density compared to the

[1] James G. Speight: The Chemistry and Technology of Petroleum. FOURTH EDITION. Taylor & Francis Group, LLC. 2007. P 135:136

Fundamentals of Petroleum and Petrochemical Engineering surrounding non-porous and hard rock layers. Thus, a gravimetric curve is acquired and analyzed for the location of deposit. [1]

1.4. Magnetic surveys

The magnetic method detects changes in the earth's magnetic field caused by variations in the magnetic properties of rocks. In particular, basement and igneous rocks are relatively highly magnetic. If they are located close to the surface they give rise to anomalies with a short wavelength and high amplitude. The method is airborne (plane or satellite) which permits rapid surveying and mapping with good areal coverage. Like the gravity technique this survey is often employed at the beginning of an exploration venture. [2]

Magnetic methods are based upon measuring the magnetic effects produced by varying concentrations of ferromagnetic minerals, such as magnetite. Instruments used for magnetic prospecting vary from the simple

---

[1] Uttam Ray Chaudhuri: Fundamentals of Petroleum and Petrochemical Engineering. Taylor and Francis Group. 2011. P 9

[2] Frank Jahn, Mark Cook and Mark Graham: HYDROCARBON EXPLORATION AND PRODUCTION. 2ND EDITION. Elsevier B.V. 2008. P 26

mining compass used in the seventeenth century to sensitive airborne magnetic units permitting intensity variations to be measured with an accuracy greater than 1=10,000 part of the earth's field.

The magnetometer is a specially designed magnetic compass and detects minute differences in the magnetic properties of rock formations, thus helping to find structures that might contain oil, such as the layers of sedimentary rock that may lie on top of the much denser igneous, or basement, rock. The data give clues to places that might conceal anticlines or other oil favorable structures. Of even more value is the determination of the approximate total thickness of the sedimentary rock, which can save unwarranted expenditure later or more costly geophysics or even the drilling of a well when the sediment may not contain sufficient oil to warrant further investigation. Most magnetometer surveys used now are performed by the use of aircraft, which permits large-scale surveys to be made rapidly and surveys over regions that may be otherwise inaccessible.

One of the most widely used magnetic instruments is the Schmidt vertical magnetometer. It consists of a pair of blade magnets balanced horizontally on a quartz knife edge. The balance is oriented at right angles to the magnetic meridian. The deflection from the horizontal is observed, giving the variation in magnetic vertical intensity with gravity. The torsion fiber magnetometer is also a vertical component instrument but has an operating range greater than the Schmidt instrument. It also has an advantage in that it is easier and quicker to read.

The instrument values are referred to a base and corrected for temperature and diurnal variation and for the normal geographic variation of the earth's magnetic field. The nuclear precession magnetometer is another continuous recording magnetic instrument that measures the earth's total magnetic field by observing the free precession (progressive movement) frequency of the protons in a sample of water.

The interpretation of magnetic measurements is subject to the same fundamental drawbacks as noted for gravity measurements. The drawbacks are as follows:

1. Contrast in physical properties of the formations

2. Depth of origin and integrated contributions from many sources

3. Changes in strength and direction of the earth's field with location

4. Canceling effect related to proximity of opposite induced poses at the boundaries of finite geological bodies

However, the method has proved valuable in exploration for magnetic mineral deposits, in the determination of geological structural trends, and in estimating the probable depth of the crystalline rock floor beneath sedimentary rock areas. [1]

Earth has its own magnetic field that varies from one location to another owing to the different structural materials of rocks and also the presence of solar-charged particles received by Earth. A variation of magnetic field strength is recorded by a sensitive instrument, called a magnetometer. Igneous non-porous rocks are found to be magnetic as compared to sedimentary rocks containing organic deposits.

Thus, a magneto metric survey can also be used to locate oil deposits. Both the gravimetric and magneto metric methods are done simultaneously to predict a reproducible sub-surface structure. After the zone is confirmed by gravimetric and magneto metric surveys, a seismic survey is carried out for a clear image of the sub-surface structure. [2]

---

[1] James G. Speight: The Chemistry and Technology of Petroleum. FOURTH EDITION. Taylor & Francis Group, LLC. 2007. P 136:137

Electromagnetic methods are based upon the concept that an alternating magnetic field causes an electrical current to flow in conducting material. Measurements are carried out by connecting a source of alternating current to a coil of wire, which acts as a source for a magnetic field similar to that which will be produced by a short magnet located on the axis of the coil. A receiving system consisting of a second coil connected to a voltmeter is mounted, so that there is free rotation about a horizontal axis.

The receiving coil should be mounted so that rotation is on an axis perpendicular to that of the induced magnetic field. In this case, the induced voltage (in the absence of a conductor) will vary from zero (when the coil plane is parallel to the plane of the applied field) to a maximum (when the coil plane is perpendicular to the plane of the applied field). However, if a conductor is present, the induced current in the conductor sets up a secondary magnetic field that distorts the primary field and gives a value that is not horizontal except directly over the conductor. By using an inclinometer to record the angle of the moving search coil when in the null position, the location of a conductor can be determined as the

---

[2] Uttam Ray Chaudhuri: Fundamentals of Petroleum and Petrochemical Engineering. Taylor and Francis Group. 2011. P 10

crossover (inflection) point on a profile across the body.

Another variation of this method is to have both the receiver and the transmitting coils in the horizontal plane. In this arrangement, the voltage developed over nonconducting ground is a function of the construction of the coils that are usually moved across the ground with a constant separation. The presence of a conductor is indicated by changes in the voltage values from the normal values for this configuration. [1]

1.5. ELECTRICAL METHODS

Electrical prospecting methods depend upon differences in electrical conductivity between the geological bodies under study and the surrounding rocks. In general, metallic minerals, particularly the sulfides, range in resistivity from 1.0 to several Ω-cm, whereas consolidated sediments of low water content average about 10^4 S-cm, igneous rocks range from 10^4 to 10^6 Ω-cm, and saturated unconsolidated sediments from 10^2 to 10^4 Ω-cm. The resistivity of the last depends largely on the amount and electrolytic nature (salinity) of the included water.

---

[1] James G. Speight: The Chemistry and Technology of Petroleum. FOURTH EDITION. Taylor & Francis Group, LLC. 2007. P 138:139

On the other hand, the self-potential method makes use of the fact that most metallic sulfide minerals are easily oxidized by downward-percolating groundwater. As a result of this surface oxidation, the elements of a simple chemical battery are established and an electrical current flow down through the ore body and back to the surface through the surrounding water-saturated ground, which acts as the electrolyte. It is possible to locate these localized electrical fields and, hence, ore bodies by mapping points of equal electrical potential at the surface using nonpolarizing electrodes and a sensitive ammeter, or a milli-ammeter. Alternatively, measuring the potential differences between successive profile stakes forming a grid over an area using a potentiometer can also be employed.

A special application of electrical methods is in the study of subsurface stratigraphy by measuring the potential differences between the surface and an electrode lowered in a borehole and also by measuring variations in electrical resistivity with depth (electrical logging). This method produces a measure of porosity and permeability, as the data are affected markedly by the ability of the drilling fluid to penetrate the formation. The resistivity measurements define the position of formation boundaries and the lithological character of the sediments.

Three resistivity logs are usually taken: (1) one having a shallow penetration to define the location of the formation boundaries and two others having (2) intermediate and (3) deep penetration. These last two logs are used to determine the extent to which the drilling fluid has penetrated into the formations and the true resistivity of the formation present. The various measurements taken in conjunction provide a valuable tool not only for studying conditions in a given well, but also for carrying out correlation studies between wells and thus defining geological structure and horizontal changes in lithology. [1]

1.6. RADIOACTIVE METHODS

In the disintegration of radioactive minerals three spontaneous emissions take place, the election of an electron (β-ray), a helium nucleus (α-ray), and short-wavelength electromagnetic radiation (¥-rays). The instruments used in radioactive exploration are the Geiger counter and the scintillometer. In addition to prospecting for radioactive minerals, the radioactive method is extensively applied in borehole studies of subsurface stratigraphy as might be deemed necessary when prospecting for oil. Different sedimentary rocks are naturally characterized by different concentrations of

[1]James G. Speight: The Chemistry and Technology of Petroleum. FOURTH EDITION. Taylor & Francis Group, LLC. 2007. P 138

radioactive materials. Shale and volcanic ash give the highest g-ray count and limestone, the lowest ¥-ray count. [1]

1.7. CSEM seabed logging

Controlled source electro-magnetic (CSEM) surveying or seabed logging is a remote sensing technique which uses very low frequency electro-magnetic signals emitted from a source near the seabed. Receivers are placed on the

---

[1] James G. Speight: The Chemistry and Technology of Petroleum. FOURTH EDITION. Taylor & Francis Group, LLC. 2007. P 139

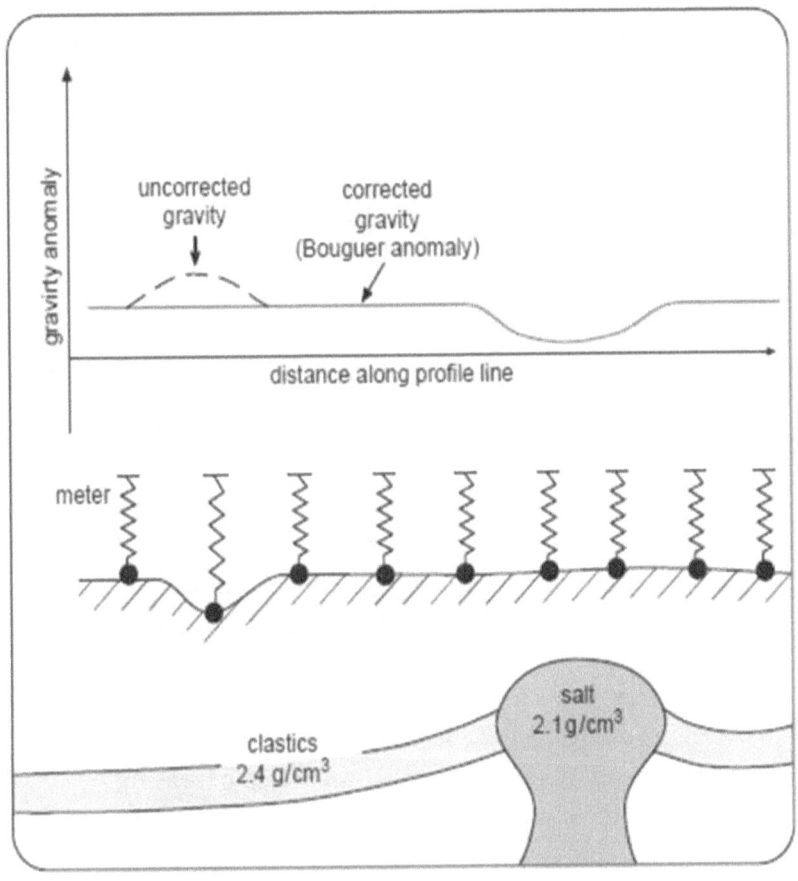

seabed at regular intervals and register anomalies and distortions in the electromagnetic signal generated by resistive bodies, such as reservoirs saturated with hydrocarbons.

CSEM works best in deep water (W500 m) in areas characterized by relatively simple sand-shale sequences (clastic reservoirs); it is particularly useful for surveying large traps (prospects) where other marine methods are less practical or economical.

It is being increasingly used in conjunction with seismic data to verify likely fluid fill within the reservoir rocks of a prospect, thus helping to reduce risk and to improve the chance of success by allowing wells to be targeted in a more sophisticated way. [1]

1.8. REMOTE SENSING METHOD

Solar radiation from the Earth's surface varies in intensity and frequency depending on the sub-surface property. This observation is collected via satellite to predict the sub-surface structure. In order to image the sub-surface structure, historical geological data collected previously by gravimetric, magneto metric, and seismic surveys are used. The final image is obtained by geological imaging software (GIS). However, the remote sensing method is not applicable during nighttime or places incapable of reflecting solar radiation, like the ocean surface, which absorbs substantial amounts of solar radiation. However, extrapolation from the land surface in the vicinity of the sea can be accurately predicted but is not applicable for the deep-sea area. A

---

[1]Frank Jahn, Mark Cook and Mark Graham: HYDROCARBON EXPLORATION AND PRODUCTION. 2ND EDITION. Elsevier B.V. 2008. P 26: 27

radioactive or gamma-ray survey is also used in the exploration.

1.9. GEOCHEMICAL METHODS

Inorganic contents of surface or shallow cuttings or core are sampled and analyzed for inorganic materials, such as salts and carbonates, which are frequently associated with hydrocarbons. *Organic contents* or the presence of organic matter is detected by heating a sample in a crucible and the loss of mass of the sample is an indication of the presence of organic matter. The ratio of organic mass to inorganic matter in a sample is used to ascertain the presence of hydrocarbons. *Total organic carbon* is defined as the carbon present in the organic matter in the sample which is different in inorganic carbon from carbonates. Core samples are examined for porosity, permeability, salt content, organic content, and many other physical and chemical properties. [1]

1.10. STRATIGRAPHY

Correlations are established between wells, fossils, rock and mud properties, before and during drilling operations for the final prediction, and this technique is known as stratigraphy. But it is important to remember that prediction from exploration may not be correct

---

[1] Uttam Ray Chaudhuri: Fundamentals of Petroleum and Petrochemical Engineering. Taylor and Francis Group. 2011. P 11

as far as the location and amount of deposit are concerned. It may happen that the drilling operation may not yield oil or the yield may not be sufficient at the explored site and that the expenditure borne by this work is irrecoverable. Hence, a more accurate determination of the location and economic deposit should be done before investing money in well construction. After confirmation from the test drilled hole, final construction is carried out. [1]

1.11. LIBS Technique for Identification of Crude Oils

The motivation for the detection of trace elements in crude oil is oil exploitation and its quality determination, if possible in-situ. Therefore, information on trace elements is increasingly important for the characterization of crude oil and to take corrective measures during production and its refinement.

Elemental analysis of a crude oil is performed to determine the presence and content of various elements such as C, H, O, S. N, Ni, V, Fe, etc. The first five elements are part of the matrix, while the others are considered impurities and their oil content is in the order of the traces. [2]

---

[1]Uttam Ray Chaudhuri: Fundamentals of Petroleum and Petrochemical Engineering. Taylor and Francis Group. 2011. P 11

Atomic absorption (AA) spectroscopy and plasma generated by inductive coupling (ICP-AES) are the most used techniques for the determination of trace elements. However, these methods have a number of drawbacks such as: use of expensive solvents, digestion processes, contamination with reactive, use of hazardous reagents, etc.

LIBS is a technique of atomic emission spectroscopy firmly established for rapid determination of the elemental composition of matter represented in any state of aggregation. This technique allows elemental analysis with a large number of advantages, among them the use of fiber optics and lenses, which allow to direct and collect radiation from places otherwise inaccessible; which makes it particularly attractive for the analysis of hazardous materials, at high temperatures, or for working in harsh environments. Furthermore, as the laser acts as sampling and excitation source, can be analyzed virtually all kinds of samples whether conductive or not, regardless of the state of aggregation in which they are. Additionally, the result is delivered quickly and in principle the

---

[2]Amalia Martı́nez-Garcı́a • Cosme Furlong • Bernardino Barrientos • Ryszard J. Pryputniewicz: Emerging Challenges for Experimental Mechanics in Energy and Environmental Applications, Proceedings of the 5th International Symposium on Experimental Mechanics and 9th Symposium on Optics in Industry (ISEM-SOI), 2015. Springer International Publishing Switzerland 2017. P 181

equipment may have the necessary degree of portability required for in-situ analysis. [1]

In recent years, the LIBS technique has been successfully used for the rapid analysis of multi-elemental contaminants in solid matrix. LIBS can be useful for the analysis of liquid and solid samples in a variety of applications such as industrial materials analysis, prospecting and mining, environmental monitoring, national security measures, chemical and biological agents, forensics, pharmaceutical research and development.

LIBS has found utility in monitoring elementary processes and in field portable analyzers for in situ analysis of real samples traces, where accuracy and precision are not the primary requirement.

In the case of compositional analysis of crude oil, although previous reports can be found, it is work done with expensive laser equipment and, moreover, spectra show an intense electronic background caused by sample conditions, that limits sensibility. [2]

---

[1] Amalia Martı́nez-Garcı́a • Cosme Furlong • Bernardino Barrientos • Ryszard J. Pryputniewicz: Emerging Challenges for Experimental Mechanics in Energy and Environmental Applications, Proceedings of the 5th International Symposium on Experimental Mechanics and 9th Symposium on Optics in Industry (ISEM-SOI), 2015. Springer International Publishing Switzerland 2017. P 181
[2] Amalia Martı́nez-Garcı́a • Cosme Furlong • Bernardino

1.12. SEISMIC SURVEY

This technique uses a sonic instrument over a desired site to correctly locate the prospective basin structure. In this method, a sound signal generated by the explosion method (explorers call them mini-earthquakes, which are artificially created by explosives) is transmitted through the earth's surface under study and reflected signals are detected by geophones located at specified positions. The frequency and time of the reflected signal varies with the density, porosity, and the type of reflecting surface. Various rock deposits at different depths vary with density and porosity.

Seismic reflection can measure this change as it travels below the surface. Computer simulation software is used for imaging the sub-surface structure. This is applied to all the surveys for fast and accurate prediction about the oil and gas reserve location, well before a site is finally selected for drilling operations. It is to be noted that exploration has to be deterministic, but the availability of oil and gas is estimated based on probability. [1]

Barrientos • Ryszard J. Pryputniewicz: Emerging Challenges for Experimental Mechanics in Energy and Environmental Applications, Proceedings of the 5th International Symposium on Experimental Mechanics and 9th Symposium on Optics in Industry (ISEM-SOI), 2015. Springer International Publishing Switzerland 2017. P 181
([1])Uttam Ray Chaudhuri: Fundamentals of Petroleum and Petrochemical Engineering. Taylor and Francis Group. 2011. P 10

Seismic methods are based on determinations of the time interval that elapses between the initiation of a sound wave from detonation of a dynamite charge or other artificial shock and the arrival of the vibration impulses at a series of seismic detectors (geophones). The arrivals are amplified and recorded along with time marks (0.01 sec intervals) to give the seismogram.

The method depends upon whether (1) the velocity within each of the layers penetrated at depth is greater than that in the layers above; (2) the layers are bounded by plane surfaces; and (3) the material within each layer is essentially homogeneous.

The seismograph measures the shock waves from explosions initiated by triggering small controlled charges of explosives at the bottom of shallow holes in the ground. The formation depth is determined by the time elapsed between the explosion and detection of the reflected wave at the surface.

The depths and media reached by seismic waves depend on the distance between shot point and receiving points. The first impulses or breaks in a seismogram are caused by waves that have traveled quickly between the shot point and any receiving point. At short distances this is usually also the shortest path, but beyond a certain distance it is quicker for a refracted pulse to travel via a longer path involving underlying layers with a higher velocity. From a plot of travel time as a function of surface distance, data are obtained for determining both the velocity of the material and number of layers present. From the distances at which changes in velocity are indicated, the depth of each layer can be computed.

In general, the deeper, older formations as a result of higher compression have a higher density and also a higher seismic velocity than the overlying material. Observed differences in velocity not only define the direction of slope of the rock surfaces but also provide information for computing the degree of slope present. For what might be termed normal conditions (increase in velocity with depth), the error determined in depths is usually less than 10% with this method.

Seismic geophysical work is also carried out on the water, greatly aiding the search for oil on the continental shelves and other areas covered by water. A marine seismic project moves continually, with detectors towed behind the boat at a constant speed and a fairly constant depth. Explosive charges are detonated at a position and time determined by the speed of the boat, so that a continuous survey of the reflecting horizons can be obtained. [1]

---

[1] James G. Speight: The Chemistry and Technology of

Advances in seismic surveying techniques and the development of more sophisticated seismic processing algorithms over the last few decades have changed the way fields are developed and managed. From being a predominantly exploration focused tool, seismic surveying has progressed to become one of the most cost-effective methods for optimizing field production. In many cases, seismic data have allowed operators to extend the life of 'mature' fields by many years.

Petroleum. FOURTH EDITION. Taylor & Francis Group, LLC. 2007. P 137

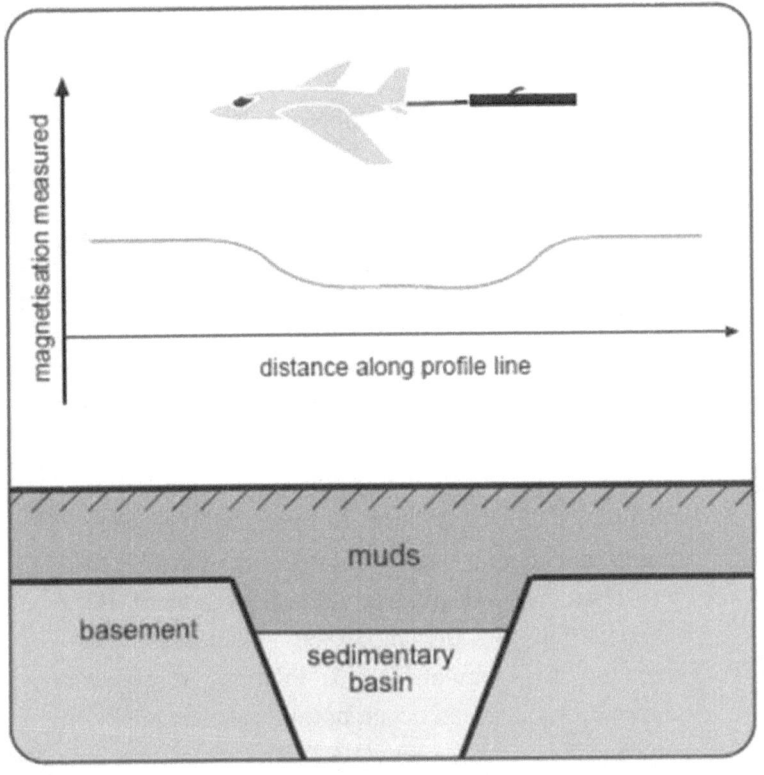

Seismic surveys involve generating sound waves which propagate through the earth's rocks down to reservoir targets. The waves are reflected to the surface, where they are registered in receivers, recorded and stored for processing. The resulting data make up an acoustic image of the subsurface which is interpreted by geophysicists and geologists.

Seismic surveying is used in

- exploration for delineating structural and stratigraphic traps

- field appraisal and development for estimating reserves and drawing up FDPs

- production for reservoir surveillance such as observing the movement of reservoir fluids in response to production.

Seismic acquisition techniques vary depending on the environment (onshore or offshore) and the purpose of the survey. In an exploration area a seismic survey may consist of a loose grid of 2D lines. In contrast, in an area undergoing appraisal, a 3D seismic survey will be shot. In some mature fields a permanent 3D acquisition network might be installed on the seabed for regular (6–12 months) reservoir surveillance, called ocean bottom stations (OBS) or ocean bottom cables (OBC). [1]

Up to the First World War, all geological knowledge was in fact exclusively based on surface indicators providing a vague clue as to the location of underground reservoirs. Throughout the USA, the most reliable signal for the oil prospector was the localization of natural eruptions like oil seepages or springs, natural gas

---

[1]Frank Jahn, Mark Cook and Mark Graham: HYDROCARBON EXPLORATION AND PRODUCTION. 2ND EDITION. Elsevier B.V. 2008. P 27: 28

springs, outcrops of sands impregnated with petroleum or bitumen, bituminous dikes, and bituminous lakes. These "eruptions" were the first feature to look for as they demonstrated that at least some oil existed in the vicinity and was able to migrate to the surface. Other sedimentary formations such as sands, sandstones, shales, and limestones were also potential though less certain clues. For field-working American geologists, this hint was nonetheless of limited relevance since the few unveiled seepages quickly got drilled by wildcatters. On the contrary, seepage search did prove very productive in countries such as Mexico and Azerbaijan—Russia where oil and gas leaked copiously from source rocks. So abundant was this type of primary surface indicators that the methodology for the second comprehensive Mexican oil survey relied chiefly on inventorying

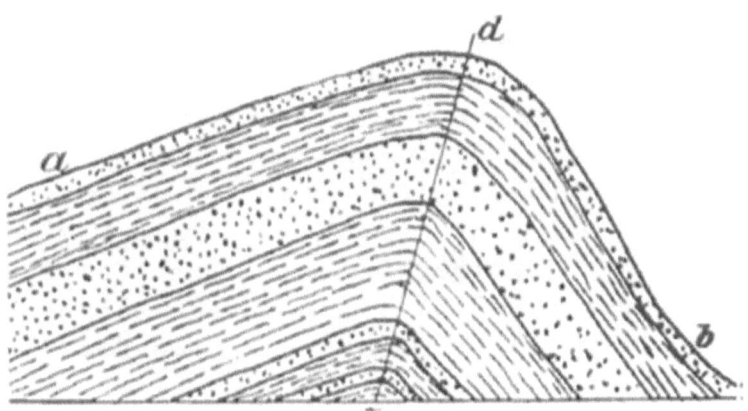

"chapopoteras" (seepages) scattered all over the country and complemented by a geological description of the underlying sedimentary rock structure. Before the 1910 revolution, the country had consolidated a hub of national oil geology expertise centered in the "small but highly respected organization" of the "Instituto Geologico de Mexico," which kept in close contact with their North American colleagues. In Azerbaijan, on the other hand, far-reaching seepages made the tapping of oil from surface wells a remunerative business for local tribes and an ecological nightmare once every amateur, adventurer, and speculator began drilling at random during the oil rush of the 1880s. In truth, drilling appeared to be the single talent required to find oil.

Finally, in the absence of any such clear-cut indicators, geological advice could do no better than recommending searching for the usual landscape fold bed surfacing in an upwards convex form, with the oldest geological beds at its core. Unlike the former empirical guidelines, this particular suggestion was grounded on a theory of oil occurrence—in fact, the most accepted epochal theory within the scientific community: the anticlinal theory of oil accumulation. This convex salience identified by the observer was likely to match a geological structure called an anticline. Anticlines are geological structures involving rock formations bent by a tectonic process into an upwards convex configuration and whose fold traps form an excellent reservoir for hydrocarbons, particularly when containing reservoir-like rocks at their core and impermeable seals on the outer layers. The hypothesis that an extended "nose" at the surface could become an underground petroleum-bearing fold aroused interest in the systematic exploration of the American countryside, bringing topography back into the arms of geology. From the common perspective, this was summed up in the unwarranted idea that "all oil is found in folds."

However, perhaps the most important contribution of the anticline theory to petroleum discovery lay in the technical innovations that accompanied it, especially the systematic observation of rock altitudes and the representation of anticlines by contour-line subsurface maps. Invented for a geological survey undertaken in Trenton, topographic contour lines represented lines in depth below sea level so that the highest points on the map were labeled with the lowest values.

By disclosing the topographical relationship between the observable landscape and concealed petroleum reservoirs, the maps triggered debate about the whereabouts of gas and oil deposits. Above all, this new scientific "gadget" proved extremely useful to impress the value of geological prospecting on both the public and companies.

As expected, geologists endeavored to play their trump card by every feasible means.

The anticline theory gained momentum as more oil was found in anticlines with oil traps than theoretically predicted. West Virginia and south-western Pennsylvania offered the best supportive evidence in this respect; conversely Ohio, Indiana, and Illinois cast serious reservations on the global validity of the theory. We know today that most of the world's oil was in effect discovered in anticline structures. However, this fact, per se, did not significantly raise the earlier probability of actually finding oil. Even when selecting anticlines as their main target, geologists of the 1920s could not single out precise location criteria. Surface indicators said little about whether or not anticlines might contain oil and gas, the number of hydrocarbons in place, where the accumulation occurred, or the configuration of structural and stratigraphic traps.

Ultimately, they could miss the spot simply because the oil was not at the top of a pronounced anticline or because the trap had an unexpected stratigraphic configuration.

Furthermore, since oil was found in a great variety of structural positions, the basic anticline hypothesis underwent many vicissitudes.

The work with surface indicators required a sizable and labor-intensive organization.

Nowhere as in the prospecting of foreign lands was this feature so remarkable. One may even say that an era of geologically inspired "invasions" began with the dawn of the twentieth century sometimes involving the overseas relocation of battalions of forty to two hundred men. This stream was fostered by planned investments made by the largest oil companies and reflected the pressure to find untapped sources of supply in the face of increasingly global competition.

Mesopotamia (1904 and 1908) Trinidad and the British West Indies (1908), Argentina (1908), Ecuador (1909), Egypt (1911), Algeria (1914), and Venezuela (1917) were the most eminent cases of success in finding oil abroad. A geological expedition to China and Formosa (1914–1916) commissioned by the Standard Oil Company of New York also suggested that there was a likelihood of discovering good reservoirs, but the advance toward the production phase stalled for political reasons. In addition to the new production regions, multinational oil companies further reinforced their presence in Canada and in Peru, leading to a new cycle of discoveries, notably in Peru. So overwhelming was this trend that even firms long skeptical about geological endeavors ended up recruiting 10, 18, 26 geologists (Persia, Anglo-Persian, 1919–1924). Given the higher costs of oil prospecting in the international arena, the massification of discovery had to be spearheaded by some new institutional form of doing business: The multinational holding company was precisely the organizational structure able to finance a multiform presence in oilfields around the world.

After the First World War, the strategic commitment of these large corporations to get hold of secure supplies by constituting buffers of private reserves intensified the scrambling for oil and for leases. Soaring prices further increased the payoffs for each dollar invested in prospection. The more proactive geological stance prompted a phase of swift technological innovation with a bet on every technique that might disclose the sedimentary layers and structures lying beyond the anticline's surfaces. Between 1919 and 1929, the core of geophysical technologies, as we currently know them, was experimented with for the first time, improved, and put to good usage.

Gravity surveys, magnetic surveys, and seismic surveys derived from the idea that variations in rock density could be mapped by measuring the way they conveyed some signal. Hence, experiments with the torsion balance, a scientific instrument devised by the Hungarian Baron von Eoetvoes, relied on the assumption that the gravitational force exerted by low density ("light") rocks found close to the surface is less than those of very dense ("heavy") rocks. By the same token, the electrical current sent by a magnetometer depicted a different magnetic "anomaly" when encountering less magnetic sedimentary rocks and when coming across highly magnetic igneous rocks, thus enabling the identification of the former where oil was more likely to be found. Last of all, a concussive sound produced at the surface, in such a way that as much of its energy as possible was directed downwards, was then partially refracted backwards with greater or lesser velocity depending on the density or compactness of the geological formations encountered.

In this echo-sounding technology, a picture could be formed by registering the way in which the velocity of vibrations changed with depth. The time taken for the sound wave to reach a seismic detector located on the surface was recorded on a strip of photographic paper. Owing to the fact that the speed of transmission was proportional to the density or compactness of the geological formation, the technique was firstly used to detect salt domes, which returned a high velocity of propagation. Later on, seismic refraction methods were improved and applied for the mapping of other rock strata.

Conceived for general scientific research in geodesy and geophysics (the Gravitational method), for iron ore prospecting (the magnetic method), and for the location of enemy artillery firing positions (the seismic method), these technologies had to be further adapted to the particularities of oil surveying. As Bowker pointed out, during the first phase of learning and adjustment, the data produced by prospecting instruments could be correlated with underground structures and those structures could sometimes be correlated with the presence of oil. Nevertheless, as of the 1920s, no link in this chain had been firmly established.

It was only through further research and practical tests, financed by oil companies such as Amerada Petroleum Company, Royal Dutch Shell and Shell's affiliate Roxana, Gulf Oil and its subsidiaries, Louisiana Land & Exploration, Calcasieu Oil, Standard Oil of New York, Humble, Pure and Louisiana, Aguila and Burmah Oil, that fundamental improvements were brought about. Within a short period of time, these investments paid off and paid off handsomely. Successful discoveries of new reservoirs in southern Texas, in the USA, Mexico, and Hungary arose from the application of gravitational methods, while discoveries in states adjoining Texas, such as Louisiana, and Mexico derived from seismic refraction methods, while new finds in Texas, as well as Venezuela and Rumania, were brought about by innovative usage of magnetic surveys and electric logs.

Afterward, the effectiveness of these gravitational and magnetic methods became increasingly associated with reconnaissance surveys and efforts to measure sediment thickness. The seismic method additionally broadened its scope and seized the general-purpose geophysical exploration market outside of Texas, largely on account of its reliability, cost-benefit advantages, and enhanced opportunity "for securing preferred acreage over mapped structures.

The trend that turned seismic methods into the bedrock of core oil prospection activities was further reinforced by two international developments: First, the boom in offshore exploration that began in the late 1950s and was chiefly based on seismic marine surveys; in this respect, the production of waterproof microphones (hydrophones) deployed along a cable or a steamer proved to be, far and away, the cheapest and most efficient technology; second, the interface with computing power which led to 3-D seismic surveys and the revolution in "the process of exploration and production, since the early 1990s." Among other aspects, 3-D surveys had the advantage of easing the identification of the optimal drilling point. [1]

1.12.1. THE SEISMIC DETECTIVES

In the past 20 years, technology has transformed the way in which the oil and gas industry acquires and processes seismic data – information produced using sound waves – but it would be nothing without the geophysicists and geologists to analyze it.

The study of rock formations lies at the heart of the industry's search for oil and gas: understand a rock's structure and you understand whether it has the potential to hold precious hydrocarbons. In the industry's earliest days, this meant mapping a region's topography and geology by hand, searching for and studying formations for clues as to what might lie beneath them. If you were lucky, you'd find actual oil seeping up from below ground. [2]

In the 1920s, though, a new technology was introduced that used sound waves to create a 'picture' of the geological structure deep below ground. Seismology would go on to revolutionize the industry's ability to 'see'

---

[1] Nuno Luis Madureira: Key Concepts in Energy. Springer International Publishing Switzerland 2014. P 114: 118

[2] BP Magazine Issue 1. 2015. P 13: 14

below the surface and, today, it is the foundation of any search for hydrocarbons.

It works by transmitting sound into the Earth and then recording the reflection – or echo – using sensors called geophones – or offshore, hydrophones. Different types of rock have different effects on the way in which a sound wave is reflected, along with its strength. Waves return as either a positive or negative reflection and sometimes the interpreter can directly infer the presence of hydrocarbons from the magnitude and polarity of these reflections. Terry Redshaw worked as a geophysicist at BP for 30 years and describes his job as being a little like a police detective. "I like to think of it as if we're accusing a piece of rock of harboring oil and gas and to do that we need to gather evidence to build a case that is strong enough for BP to invest money into drilling a prospect." [1]

Oil is lighter than water, so once generated, it will 'float' up through layers of porous and permeable rock until it either seeps out at ground level or hits an impermeable rock layer, known as a seal.

Sometimes, the combined geometry of the seal and reservoir forms a trap. In its most basic form, a trap can be a concave downward fold or dome – rather like an upside-down bowl.

---

[1]BP Magazine Issue 1. 2015. P 14

This trap prevents the hydrocarbons from rising farther. Spot these formations on a piece of seismic and you have your first clues.

"We have an expression in exploration, 'thinking like a molecule'," says Redshaw, "so we're trying to figure out where might hydrocarbon molecules hide? We look for certain elements – a source rock that produces hydrocarbons and a seal that prevents them from floating higher. We can also sometimes see how the seismic response changes depending on the fluid that is in there – for example, water behaves differently from gas, which behaves differently from oil." [1]

1.12.2. 3D SEISMIC

During the 1980s, the industry began to develop and use 3D seismic technology, marking another dramatic change in the way geoscientists could see subsurface rock formations. 3D seismic is created by sending multiple soundwaves under the ground from closely spaced lines, so as to provide an image taken from many points to ensure dense surface coverage.

The efficiency and angle of this coverage are key aspects of designing seismic surveys and BP has developed several new techniques over the past decade.

---

[1]BP Magazine Issue 1. 2015. P 14: 15

For example, BP developed a technique for onshore seismic studies using simultaneous source trucks to survey large areas more efficiently – in the past, these trucks had to move in the same direction and vibrate at the same time in order to not distort the returning sound waves.

With this new technique, the trucks move and vibrate independently. Meanwhile, offshore BP has developed a technique called 'wide azimuth towed streamers' (WATS), which uses a conventional seismic vessel with streamers of receivers towed behind it, along with additional vessels acting as offset source boats, to collect the reflected sound waves. This technique has helped BP to create images of difficult areas by ensuring a large number of potential reflection pathways between sources, horizon of interest and receiver. In other words, while 2D gives you an outline, 3D fills in the gaps.

Redshaw says: "With 2D, you don't know what is happening between one seismic line and another. However, a lot could be happening in the rock. Because we have so many more lines in 3D, you can start to look at the data from any angle you like, or even get a complete view all the way around a structure. You can also build maps on top of reservoirs and look at amplitudes and detailed faults within the reservoirs."

This image (above left) is an example of a piece of 3D data. The blue, green and purple lines represent wells that have been drilled. Within the structure itself, different colors – or amplitudes – represent different reflection strengths.

"In this image, red is usually the strongest amplitude and purple the weakest," says Redshaw. "The yellow and green could indicate gas, as this gives a brighter reflection than oil. The blue here probably indicates water."

The position of potential water in a reservoir is just as important as where the oil and gas might be. "It's useful to know where the water is and how much might be down there. A large aquifer located near a hydrocarbon trap could help to keep up pressures in the reservoir as you extract the oil and gas, so long as there is good 'communication' between the rock pores to allow movement. The position of water also allows you to determine where to place water injection wells, should you need to improve reservoir pressure."

Using 2D and 3D together, geoscientists can start to make judgements on how much oil and gas might be in place – in other words, how big the container is. "In order to drill, we have to be able to say there is a structure in place and estimate how big that structure might be," says Redshaw. "You need to map the overall container. The 2D gives me an idea of the container's shape, while 3D gives me the scale of that container – its walls, essentially." [1]

1.12.3. 4D SEISMIC

The latest developments in seismic technology have added a fourth dimension to the available data – time. By reshooting seismic at regular intervals over a field's life, a new picture starts to form that shows geoscientists how a reservoir is behaving.

When oil is taken out of a reservoir, the pressure drops and fluids move to readjust. If the reservoir is connected to an aquifer, then the water levels might rise to counteract that pressure drop. you might expect to see your blue areas rising and your red, green and yellow areas getting smaller. This movement allows you to make decisions about if, when and where to drill further wells. Redshaw explains: "Using 4D seismic helps us manage our reservoirs more effectively, deciding where to put our producing wells, our water injection wells, and how many, all in order to maintain production levels over the life of the field." [2]

([1])BP Magazine Issue 1. 2015. P 17

Seismic surveys can be repeated at difference times over the course of field life, for example at regular intervals after production has started. Changes in seismic amplitude and other attributes may occur on the post-production seismic data (monitor survey) when compared to the original pre-production seismic data (baseline survey). These changes are usually related to fluid movement and changes in fluid content as a result of depleting a reservoir.

Time-lapse seismic data can include repeat VSP surveys, 2D surveys or 3D surveys, the latter are termed '4D' data. Time-lapse surveys are becoming increasingly popular especially in mature fields where 4D data can highlight the presence of unswept compartments or track the movement of flood

---

(²)BP Magazine Issue 1. 2015. P 17

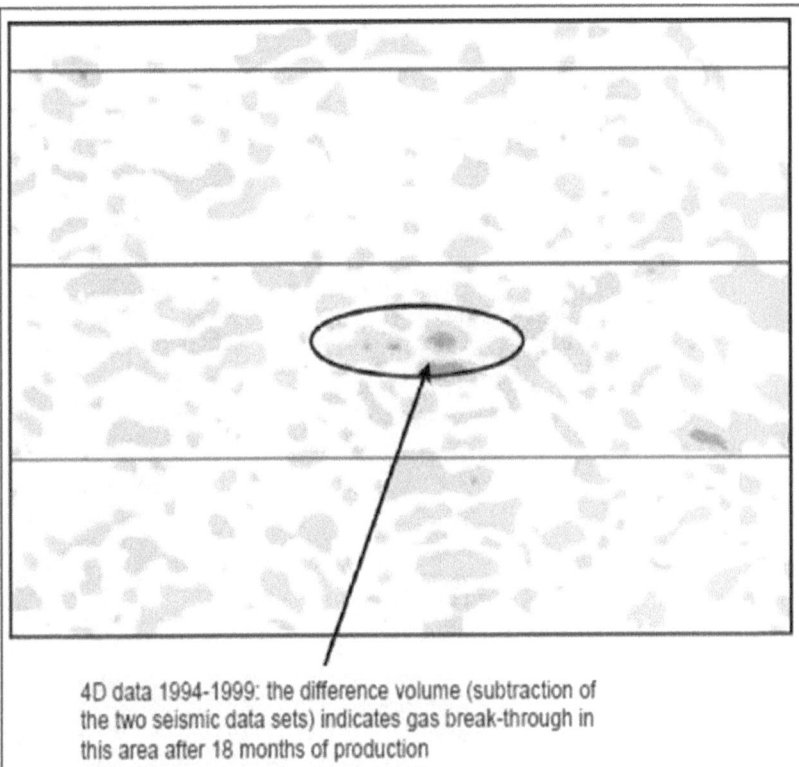

4D data 1994-1999: the difference volume (subtraction of the two seismic data sets) indicates gas break-through in this area after 18 months of production

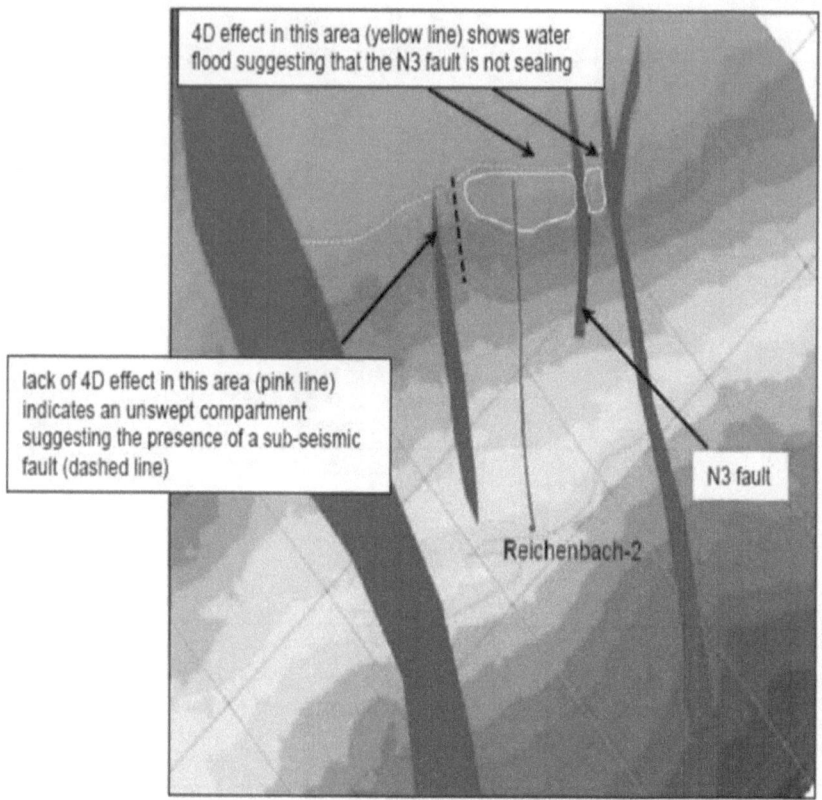

Top Lower Reservoir map (Conan turbidite series) with areas of 4D changes shown

fronts. Obviously, in areas where there is a permanent seismic acquisition system (OBC) the cost of acquiring the repeat survey(s) is much reduced. [1]

---

[1] Frank Jahn, Mark Cook and Mark Graham: HYDROCARBON EXPLORATION AND PRODUCTION. 2ND EDITION. Elsevier B.V. 2008. P 45: 46

1.12.4. Seismotectonics and Seismic Structure

The Arabian Peninsula forms a single tectonic plate, the Arabian Plate. It is surrounded on all sides by active plate boundaries as evidenced by earthquake locations. Figure shows a map of the Arabian Peninsula along with major tectonic features and earthquake locations.

Active tectonics of the region is dominated by the collision of the Arabian Plate with the Eurasian Plate along the Zagros and Bitlis Thrust systems, rifting and seafloor spreading in the Red Sea and Gulf of Aden. Strike-slip faulting occurs along the Gulf of Aqabah and Dead Sea Transform fault systems. The great number of earthquakes in the Gulf of Aqabah poses a significant seismic hazard to Saudi Arabia. Large earthquakes in the Zagros Mountains of southern Iran may lead to long-period ground motion in eastern Saudi Arabia.

The two large regions associated with the presence or absence of a sedimentary cover define the large scale geologic structure of the Arabian Peninsula. The Arabian Platform (eastern Arabia) is covered by sediments that thicken toward the Arabian Gulf. The Arabian Shield has no appreciable sedimentary cover with many outcrops. The northwestern regions of Saudi Arabia are distinct from the Arabian Shield, as this region is characterized by high seismicity in the Gulf of Aqabah and Dead Sea Rift. Active tectonics in this region is associated with the opening of the northern Red Sea and Gulf of Aqabah as well as a major continental strike-slip plate boundary.

The Dead Sea transform system connects active spreading centers of the Red Sea to the area where the Arabian Plate is converging with Eurasia in southern Turkey. The Gulf of Aqabah in the southern portion of the rift system has experienced left-lateral strike-slip faulting with a 110 km offset since early Tertiary to the present. The seismicity of the Dead Sea transform is characterized by both swarm and mainshock-aftershock types of earthquake activities.

Petroleum Exploration

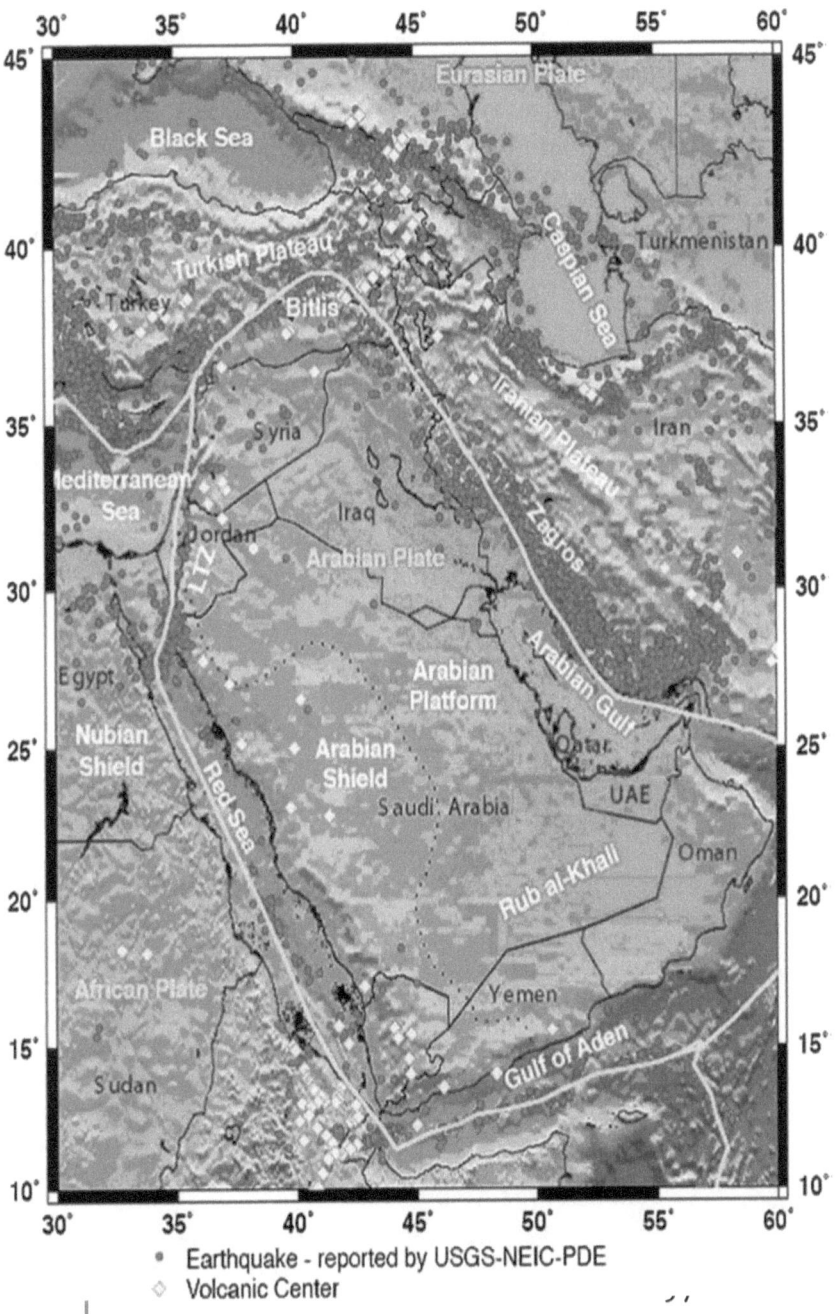

The Arabian Plate boundary extends east-northeast from the Afar region through the Gulf of Aden and into the Arabian Sea and Zagros fold belt. The boundary is clearly delineated by tele seismic epicenters, although there are fewer epicenters bounding the eastern third of the Arabian Plate south of Oman. Most seismicity occurs in the crustal part of the Arabian Plate beneath the Zagros folded belt. The Zagros is a prolific source of large magnitude earthquakes with numerous magnitude 7+ events occurring in the last few decades. The overall lack of seismicity in the interior of the Arabian Peninsula suggests that little internal deformation of the Arabian Plate is presently occurring. Mooney et al. (1985) suggest that the geology and velocity structure of the Shield can be explained by a model in which the Shield developed in the Precambrian by suturing of island arcs. They interpreted the boundary between the eastern shield and the Arabian Platform as a suture zone between crustal blocks of differing composition. Surface waves observed at the long-period analog stations RYD (Riyadh), SHI (Shiraz, Iran), TAB (Tabriz, Iran), HLW (Helwan, Egypt), AAE (Addis-Ababa, Ethiopia) and JER (Jerusalem) were used to estimate crustal and upper mantle structure, These studies reported faster crustal velocities for the Arabian Shield and slower velocities for the Arabian Platform.

The Saudi Arabian Broadband Deployment provided the first data set of broadband recordings of this region. This deployment consisted of nine broadband three-component seismic stations along a similar transect an early seismic refraction study. Data from the experiment resulted in several studies and models. These studies provided new constraints on crustal and upper mantle structure. The crustal model of the western Arabian Platform shows a little higher P-velocity for the upper crust in the Shield than in the Platform and the crustal Platform seems to have a greater thickness than in the Shield by about 3 km. The Moho discontinuity beneath the western Arabian Platform indicates a velocity of 8.2 km/sec of the upper mantle and 42 km depth.

Generally, the crustal thickness in the Arabian Shield area varies from 35 to 40 km in the west adjacent to the Red Sea to 45 km in central Arabia. Not surprising the crust thins nears the Red Sea. High-frequency regional S-wave phases are quite different for paths sampling the Arabian Shield than those sampling the Arabian Platform. In particular the mantle Sn phase is nearly absent for paths crossing parts of the Arabian Shield, while the crustal Lg phase is extremely large amplitude.

This may result from an elastic propagation effect or extremely high mantle attenuation and low crustal attenuation occurring simultaneously, or a combination of both.

Previous reports of large scale seismic structure suggest that a low velocity anomaly in the upper mantle extends laterally beneath the Arabian Shield from the Red Sea in the west to the shield—platform boundary in the east. Additionally, Debayle et al. (2001) observe a narrow region of low velocity beneath the Red Sea and western edge of the Arabian Shield, extending to 650 km depth. A recent tomographic velocity model and receiver function analysis by (Benoit et al. 2002) suggests the upper mantle low velocity anomaly is smaller in extent, laterally and vertically, than imaged in previous studies. [1]

1.12.5. Seismic Noise Measurements

Background seismic noise is an unavoidable problem in earthquake monitoring. The amplitudes of seismic arrivals decrease with distance and seismic magnitude. Path propagation effects, such as attenuation and elastic structure lead to variability in seismic amplitudes. Noise inhibits the detection of weak seismic arrivals (phases) from distant and/or small events. Seismic noise is generated from a

---

[1] Khalid Al Hosani • Francois Roure • Richard Ellison • Stephen Lokier: Lithosphere Dynamics and Sedimentary Basins: The Arabian Plate and Analogues. Springer-Verlag Berlin Heidelberg 2013. P P 281: 283

variety of sources. These include both manmade (e.g. roads, machinery) and natural sources (e.g. wind, ocean waves, temperature effects). Noise properties can vary between daylight and night hours and between seasons (e.g. summer and winter). Also, the geologic character of the seismometer placement has great effect on the noise–hard rock sites typically have lower Location map of KACST digital seismic network noise levels than sites on weathered or sedimentary rock or unconsolidated material. Because of the variety of noise sources and the variability of noise, propagation and site characteristics at network sites, the noise properties at seismic stations are frequency dependent and can be highly variable between sites.

Noise spectra were measured at KACST stations (AFFS, HASS, HILS, QURS and TATS). Event-segmented data were previewed and first arriving P-waves were picked. Waveforms were instrument corrected to absolute ground motion using the LLNL developed Seismic Analysis Code (SAC). Noise segments were taken as the available waveform before the

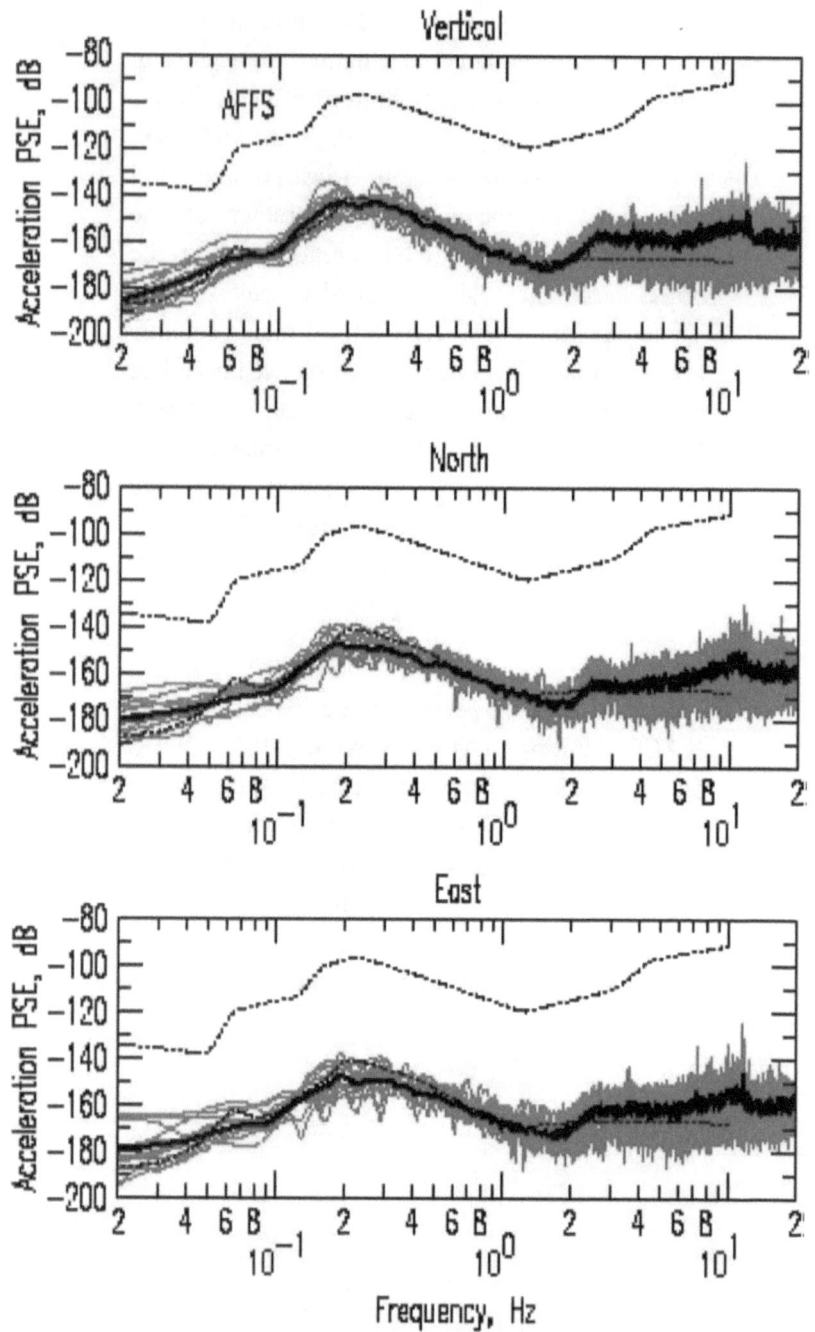

P-wave pick. Typically for SANDSN data this was 30–60 s. For noise spectral measurements we accepted only segments 30 s or longer. This limited the low-frequency resolution of our noise estimates. Power spectral densities were computed for noise windows by Fast Fourier Transform (FFT) and normalized by the window length. Noise spectra are presented in acceleration in decibels relative 1 (m/s2)2/Hz2.

Indicatively, the noise at AFFS station is presented in Fig. showing the vertical, north and east component noise acceleration power spectra (in decibels relative to 1 m2/s4). Also shown are the average low and high noise spectra as in Peterson 1993).

Results showed that stations AFFS, HILS and TATS have the lowest noise levels. Stations HASS and QURS have the highest noise levels of the sites considered. Cultural noise appears as spikes in the power spectra at frequencies above 1 Hz. This is most notable at stations HILS (4 and 8 Hz) and QURS. These sites may be affected by nearby cultural noise sources, such as roads and human activities.

Generally, the noise is relatively low amplitude between 0.1 and 1 Hz, except for station HASS. Detection of energy at frequencies around 1 Hz is most important for P-wave arrivals used in the event location. Higher frequency energy is useful for detecting local and regional events, less than 1,000 km away. [1]

1.12.6. Seismic, Semblance Cube/Time Slice Generation

Seismic acquisition and processing are crucial techniques in petroleum exploration. Firstly, for geometrical evaluation of a prospect and to estimate hydrocarbon impregnated volumes of rock. Secondly, they play a major role in the design of exploration wells. In foothill domains, the correct positioning of exploration wells remains a significant challenge.

Surface conditions (topography, rapid lateral change of surface geology) as well as subsurface structural complexity often led to poor seismic imagery. In these conditions, it becomes a real challenge to achieve optimal location of wells targeting different objectives, especially in places where there are several mechanical discontinuities in the stratigraphy. These mechanical discontinuities may induce changes in structural shape at depth. As a consequence, seismic imaging and a good geological knowledge are mandatory.

---

[1]Khalid Al Hosani • Francois Roure • Richard Ellison • Stephen Lokier: Lithosphere Dynamics and Sedimentary Basins: The Arabian Plate and Analogues. Springer-Verlag Berlin Heidelberg 2013. P 285: 288

The association of poor quality seismic with areas of rough topography is well documented. Indeed, topography related phenomena are often cited as the first order problem.

Energy traveling away from the seismic source is scattered back into the recording spread when an abrupt change in topography is encountered. In addition, when this backscattered energy is strong and interferes with primary reflections, de-noising becomes very challenging. Finally, complex ground-roll propagation including mode conversion between surface waves and body waves results in very noisy field seismograms where primary reflections can be barely seen.

In complex geological areas, a secondary problem is caused by highly dipping strata which are very difficult to properly illuminate, and image with conventional 2D seismic. Generally, in foothills, a priori geological information, such as formation depth and mechanical stratigraphy, plays a critical role in the seismic interpretation. Field mapping and well penetrations are crucial to develop this knowledge and each improvement in this domain may have an impact on seismic imaging. Better geological control not only helps in calibrating the seismic processing but also in better defining acquisition parameters in the case of a new seismic campaign design. Considering this, each major step in the geological appreciation of an area should be followed by tests of seismic reprocessing to evaluate the impact on the imaging quality.

The Kurdistan Region of Iraq has been extensively explored in the last 10 years. After several field and drilling campaigns, it was decided to drill an undrilled structure in Central KRI. The drilling plan for this well comprised two side-track trajectories in order to maximize penetration of the different objectives. During drilling, it was decided to re-process the nearest 2D seismic line to the well in order to optimize the side-track trajectory of the first leg and to clarify different drilling scenarios for the second well leg. [1]

The seismic volume used for this study extends to 5.0 s two-way travel time (TWT). Time slices generated semblance cube at 1500, 2000, 2500 ms and 3000 m reveals significant regional structural and stratigraphic features are evident at shallow to intermediate intervals (1–3.5 s). However, these features become quite difficult to identify at deeper interval (below 3.5 s), due to poor seismic quality at such depth. [2]

[1]François Roure • Ammar A. Amin Sami Khomsi • Mansour A.M. Al Garni: Lithosphere Dynamics and Sedimentary Basins of the Arabian Plate and Surrounding Areas. Springer International Publishing AG 2017. P 187: 191

1.12.7. Well to Seismic Integration

Regional stratigraphic markers (MFSs and SBs) identified from well log sequence stratigraphy were calibrated as well-tops along well-track and displayed against seismic. This made it possible to tie these markers/surfaces to seismic events. Evidences in seismic such as reflection terminations and geometry were interpreted and used to constrain their picks. However, not all picks in the well-log sequence stratigraphic panel were adequately tied to seismic all through the area of interest. Some very old MFS and SB were not picked in all the wells especially in wells located to the distal part of the study area where they did not penetrate older units, and hence it was difficult to tie and map these older markers across faults. Similarly, very young MFS and SB which lie within the chaotic and discontinuous reflections of the Benin Formation were also difficult to map across the whole study area. Pattern recognition and basic stratigraphic and structural geology principles were used to extrapolate and map these markers across the study area. [1]

---

[2]Chidozie Izuchukwu Princeton Dim: Hydrocarbon Prospectivity in the Eastern Coastal Swamp Depo-belt of the Niger Delta Basin. 2017. P 46

[1]Chidozie Izuchukwu Princeton Dim: Hydrocarbon Prospectivity in the Eastern Coastal Swamp Depo-belt of the Niger Delta Basin. 2017. P 51: 52

1.12.8. Seismic interpretation

After processing has been completed, the data are loaded onto a workstation for interpretation by geologists and geophysicists. The workstations are powerful computers, often Linux-based with dual screen capacity to allow the interpreter to look at the data in vertical section on one screen and in map view on the other. The first step in the interpretation cycle is to 'tie' the seismic data to existing well data in order to identify what the important reflector events correspond to, for example top of the reservoir or top of the main seal. In a mature field there are typically dozens of wells to calibrate to, but in exploration areas there may only be a couple, sometimes located several kilometers away.

The main reflectors or horizons are digitized from the screen (picked) and stored in a database; the same is done for the faults. In this way the structure of the field is mapped out and potential structural or stratigraphic traps are delineated. More detailed analysis can lead to identification of the internal architecture of the reservoir interval, such as separate sand bodies within a complex channel system.

Nowadays geoscientists and engineers prefer to view seismic data not in terms of reflection data with the characteristic wavelet signature, but in terms of acoustic impedance.

This is achieved by seismic inversion, a process which removes the influence of the wavelet and represents the data in a geologically meaningful way, namely as a function of rock properties. Inversion requires careful calibration to well data and knowledge of the broad geological model of the subsurface.

Once the interpretation has been completed in the time domain, the interpreted surfaces need to be converted to depth for use in the geological and engineering model. Depth conversion again requires knowledge of the seismic velocity and any significant variations, both lateral and vertical, that may be present. There are several methods of depth conversion. A simple method is to derive seismic interval velocities for a number of key intervals and then to calculate the thickness for each interval before summing them. This method is called 'isochoring' and gives a reasonable result in areas not affected by velocity variations. Another method is to build a velocity model based on stacking velocities. In areas of complex geology, more intricate methods are required and even then, there can be large discrepancies between true depth and calculated depths. [1]

---

[1]Frank Jahn, Mark Cook and Mark Graham: HYDROCARBON EXPLORATION AND PRODUCTION. 2ND EDITION. Elsevier B.V. 2008. P 40

This involves determination of depositional environments of sediments from seismic reflection characteristics. These characteristics include reflection configuration, amplitude and continuity among others. Based on seismic reflection frequency and amplitude continuity the seismic volume were divided into various facies. These includes; (i) facies with high frequency, continuous, parallel/divergent reflection, (ii) facies with lower amplitude parallel/divergent reflection, (iii) facies comprising of chaotic, discontinuous/inclined internal reflection.

High continuity and high amplitude reflection: This reflection pattern occurs within 1.8–2.4 s in cross-lines (XLs) 1049–2525 with parallel/divergent reflection patterns and grades into a low continuity, variable amplitude facies in the eastern section. High continuity of the reflection facies suggests continuous beds deposited in a relatively widespread and uniform environment. The high amplitude reflections are interpreted as inter-bedding of shale with relatively thick sands. This indicates inter-bedding high and low energy deposits which indicates a shelf environment. This corroborates the findings of Sangree and Widmier (1979) and Posamentier and Kolla (2003).

Low amplitude reflection: This is seen between 1.0 and 1.8 s on cross-line (XL) 1049 and 2525. Low amplitude facies is an indication of zone of one predominant lithologic type and this interval corresponds to massive sand facies on the well log. According to Sangree and Widmier, this massive sand associated with low amplitude reflections tend to be near shore to fluvial sands that are transported and deposited by high energy fluvial and wave processes. Intermediate facies also exist which falls between the low and high amplitude reflections. This is known as the medium amplitude reflection.

Chaotic configuration: This is appearing as discontinuous discordant reflections at the base of the section. The chaotic configuration gradually develops within XL 443, 1394, 1805–2284, and also within 3.5–6.0 s. Chaotic configuration suggests a disordered arrangement of reflection surfaces which shows a relative high energy and variability of deposition or disruption of beds after deposition. This configuration has variably abrupt to diffuse gradational boundaries which are interpreted to be reflection deposits that have been fractures by overpressures and moved upward under the weight of overlying strata during fault displacement.

The various reflection patterns with associated reflection configuration and terminations gave insight into the definition of marine unconformity and flooding surfaces. Maximum flooding surfaces and sequence boundaries are also known as down lap and onlap surfaces respectively. These were recognized on seismic section and e. Erosional surfaces marking significant unconformities and channel base were also observed.

These unconformities also coincided with sequence boundaries mapped across the seismic section the footwall thicknesses of reflection pattern indicate the occurrence of various environments of deposition. Uniform thickness observed at the onset of lambda field area represents fluvial package, thickening (divergence dip) package also at lambda field indicates shelf delta, while thinning (convergence dip) package seen at Sigma and Omicron fields suggest shelf margin delta and slope margin environments of deposition. [1]

1.12.9. Pre-Drill Seismic Processing and Interpretation (Saudi Arabia)

The original seismic dataset for our petroleum exploration in this area was acquired in 2011 by Global Geophysical Services. The parameters that were utilized are typical of modern land seismic acquisition and enable convenient sampling of the reflected wave field:

---

[1] Chidozie Izuchukwu Princeton Dim: Hydrocarbon Prospectivity in the Eastern Coastal Swamp Depo-belt of the Niger Delta Basin. 2017. P 47: 51

Receiver Group Interval: 20 m

Source Type: Vibroseis/Dynamite

Source Interval: 40 m for Vibroseis/80 m for Dynamite

Min/Max Offsets: 30 m/6010 m Split Spread

Recording Length: 6 s

Vibro Sweep Length: 12 s

Sweep Frequency: 6–80 Hz Linear

Charge Mass: 2 kg

Hole Depth: 10 m

The processing was done with a standard workflow comprising noise reduction, statics correction using refraction tomography, velocity analysis and pre-stack time and depth migrations. A second infill set of lines was acquired in 2012 and processed with the same parameters. At that time, little structural information was available to the image processor, and the imaging parameters were not optimized to allow imaging of possible steep dips.

In particular, dip limit parameter and aperture were limited to 45° and 4000 m respectively. The studied structure appeared then as a smooth fold with little internal complexity.

The interpretation used 2D seismic time and depth data from both surveys acquired in 2011 and 2012. Initial mapping was done using the fast track Post-Stack Time Migration (PSTM). Subsequent interpretation used anisotropic Pre-Stack Depth Migration (PSDM) data for detailed prospect mapping of key stratigraphic horizons and faults.

Nearby well data, Zero-Offset Vertical Seismic Profile (VSP) (velocity data as well as check shot) and synthetic seismograms were integrated into the seismic interpretation to calibrate the acoustic response of the key seismic markers.

The proposed interpretation of the structure, from Tertiary to Triassic levels, was a simple anticline (box fold) faulted toward the NE with a slight disharmony in the Baluti Shale at the base of the Jurassic sequence. [1]

Following the acquisition of FMI data at the end of first leg, an in-house reprocessing (in collaboration with GEOTOMO) of the 2011 legacy data was launched on the nearest 2D line. As this line was located 3 km away from the well, the seismic processing improvements were qualitative by nature. The main objective was to

[1] François Roure • Ammar A. Amin Sami Khomsi • Mansour A.M. Al Garni: Lithosphere Dynamics and Sedimentary Basins of the Arabian Plate and Surrounding Areas. Springer International Publishing AG 2017. P 191

improve the image of the core and the flanks of the anticline at the Triassic level.

Efforts were therefore put forth onto two key steps: the first one was data preprocessing to enhance the signal to noise ratio (solving noise and near surface perturbation issues; Mardsen 1993) and imaging, that could be now driven by a robust geological a priori based on well data and surface geology.

The reprocessing sequence was launched with a constant interaction between the processing group, the interpreters

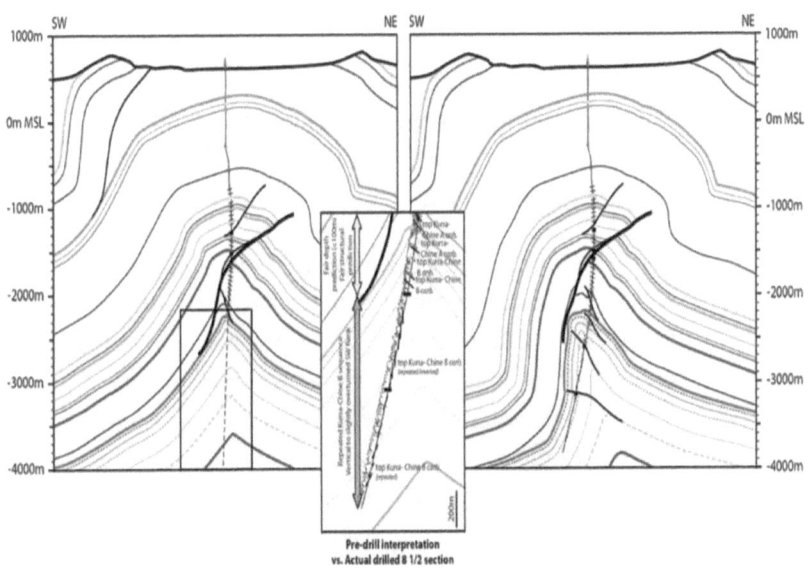
Pre-drill interpretation vs. Actual drilled 8 1/2 section

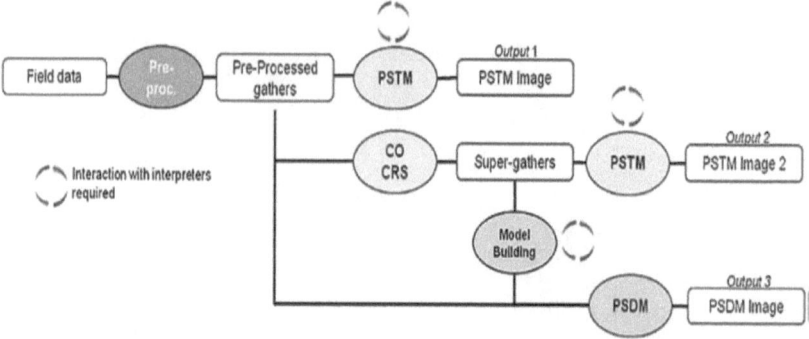

and the geologists to end up with the best imaging of the structure. This sequence can be summarized in the following four main steps:

• First, by performing a nonlinear tomography of first arrival times, and building a near surface model to correct for near surface perturbations. The quality of first-break picking is of utmost importance. Manual picking, though time-consuming, is a must;

• Second, image-based RMS velocity estimation was performed to obtain an image from Pre-Stack Time Migration (PSTM) of shot/receiver gathers, from a floating datum. Having in mind the poor data quality at target level, the classical "gather flatness" criterion alone failed to provide a robust model. Velocities were mostly picked using constant velocity scans, allowing velocity values to be chosen based of the migrated image itself, ensuring a geologically sound velocity model;

• Third, a velocity field is built layer-by-layer to obtain a Pre-Stack Depth Migration (PSDM) image from floating datum. The near surface model derived from step 1 is the starting point; below the depth of investigation of the latter (typically of the range of 500–1000 m), the model is updated iteratively layer by layer (layer-stripping) down to the depth of interest. Each layer is bounded by seismic horizons that are meaningful in terms of velocity contrast (e.g. Cretaceous— Jurassic interface), consistency from line to line also has to be assured.

• Lastly, as shown on the diagram below, the CRS tool was used as a signal enhancement technique; it provides cleaner gathers to feed the velocity building process. The CRS gathers are also migrated to provide alternative images.

The quality of the final image is equally sensitive to every step therefore each one should be carried out very carefully. In all three final steps, interaction between interpreters and the processing team is essential.

The resulting image showed clear improvements in the deep as well as in the shallow parts and showed more consistency with the geological model. In PSTM image, steep dips became to appear both in shallow and deep levels.

In addition to these less restrictive migration parameters, a fine-tuning of the velocity model was performed. As a result, nearly, vertical beds begin to appear in the PSDM image. The quality of imaging shows that the structural apexes are probably off-set with depth indicating internal disharmony in the fold in which the shallower levels (Cretaceous and Jurassic) are folded toward the NE and the deeper ones (Triassic) toward the SE.

Petroleum Exploration

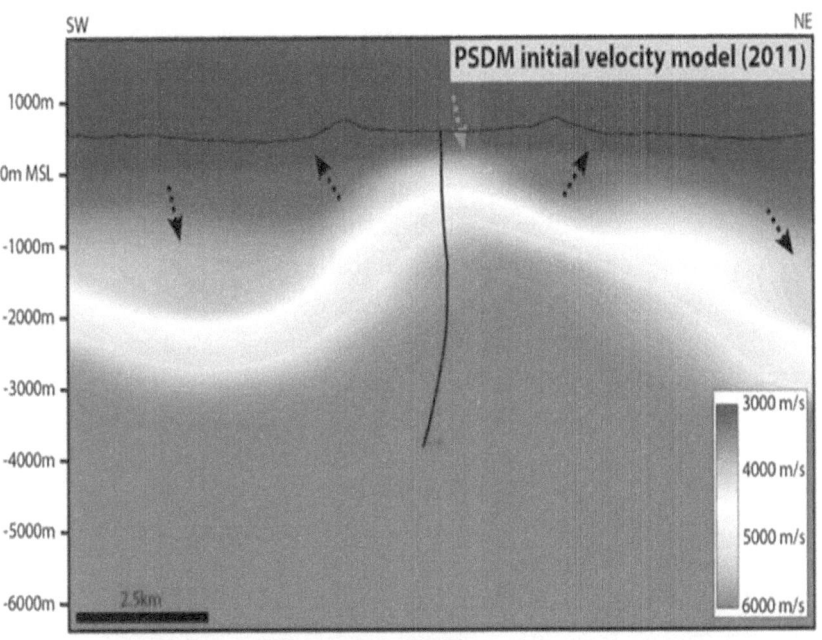

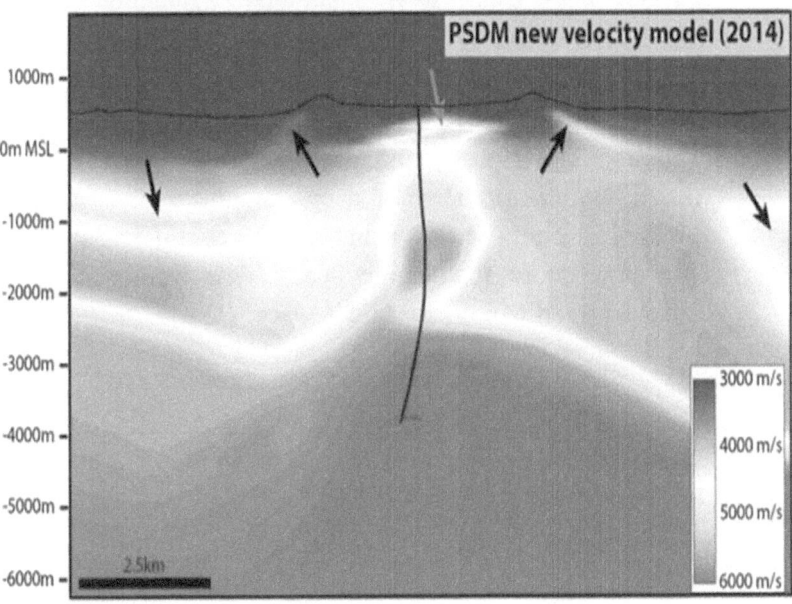

In the re-processed image, the steep dips, and the tightness of structure is can be clearly seen. The revised interpretation made for the Triassic, using these new data comprised a very pinched fold, verging toward the SW, with a relatively important disharmony in the Baluti shale, sufficient to allow a change of vergency. The remaining uncertainty was on the NE flank of the Triassic fold to know whether it is quite smooth (30–50° to the NE) or more pinched (70° to the NE). [1]

1.12.10. Fault Interpretation

Seismic volume and semblance map revealed reflection discontinuities and patterns which are identified and interpreted as faults. These fault sticks were interpreted manually using interactive 2D and 3-D windows. The fault stick picking was done systematically at very close spacing in order to get as much detail as possible. This was particularly important and quite helpful at the very deep sections of the seismic section where tracing of fault continuity becomes more challenging due to data quality deterioration with increasing depth.

Although some of the faults were linear especially the shorter ones, most of the

[1] François Roure • Ammar A. Amin Sami Khomsi • Mansour A.M. Al Garni: Lithosphere Dynamics and Sedimentary Basins of the Arabian Plate and Surrounding Areas. Springer International Publishing AG 2017. P 194: 197

interpreted sticks were large listrics faults. The bounding regional (down-to-basin) faults are mainly listric in nature and concave basin wards. They are mainly synthetic (Lambda, Sigma and Omicron fields), having the same dip direction with regional stratigraphic package, although few antithetic (counter) faults that dip against the direction of regional stratigraphic package were observed in the Kappa field. [1]

1.12.11. Horizon Interpretation

Key stratigraphic surfaces such as MFSs and SBs (horizons/events) already delineated and correlated across wells and fields all through the study area. Horizon picks were done iteratively in in-line and cross-line directions and corrected for mis-ties. In areas where reflection quality and characteristics are of good quality, lines are picked at larger intervals while at areas where reflection quality is relatively poor and characterized by discontinuities and chaotic, lines were picked at closer intervals in order to reduce mis-ties to acceptable minimum. Interpretation indicates that these stratigraphic surfaces, generally thickens from north to south (basin ward). [2]

---

[1] Chidozie Izuchukwu Princeton Dim: Hydrocarbon Prospectivity in the Eastern Coastal Swamp Depo-belt of the Niger Delta Basin. 2017. P 52
[2] Chidozie Izuchukwu Princeton Dim: Hydrocarbon Prospectivity in the Eastern Coastal Swamp Depo-belt of the Niger Delta Basin. 2017. P 52

1.12.12. Possibility to Trigger Seismic Activities on shale gas

A less visible, yet more vigilant risk of unconventional gas production is the potential seismic effect of hydraulic fracturing. Potential risks to trigger tectonic activities have been argued by some seismologists and environmental institutions, since the fracking takes place deep underground. In few European Union member states, this claim is taken seriously and led political authorities to cancel the licenses and to put shale gas production projects on a shelf. There are conflicting views on the causal effect of fracking on triggering an earthquake. However, in countries with frequent tectonic activities, even the slightest possibility has to be ruled out before stepping forward in unconventional production. [1]

Instances of earthquakes have been linked to unconventional shale gas production, for example the Cuadrilla shale gas operations near Blackpool in the UK in 2011 where a small magnitude of around two on the Richter scale was reported but did not create any surface damage.

Hydraulic fracturing operations at Cuadrilla did not lead to a moratorium to more

---

[1] Ali Nezihi Bilge • Ayhan Özgür Toy Mehmet Erdem Günay: Energy Systems and Management. Springer International Publishing Switzerland 2015. P 93

safety by the use of micro-seismic monitoring. Operators are required to implement a "traffic light" to identify unusual seismic activities that may require them to stop activities pending reassessment of operation due to hydraulic fracturing. [1]

2. Exploratory Drilling

The data collected from the geologic and geophysical surveys are used to formulate probable definitions and realizations of the geologic structure that may contain oil or gas. However, we still have to determine whether petroleum exists in these geologic traps, and if it does exist, would it be available in such a quantity that makes the development of the oil/gas field economical? The only way to provide a definite answer is to drill and test exploratory wells.

The exploratory well, known as the wildcat well, is drilled in a location determined by the geologists and geophysicists. The well is drilled with insufficient data available about the nature of the various rock layers that will be drilled or the fluids and pressures that may exist in the various formations. Therefore, the well completion and the drilling program are usually

---

[1] Joseph Tawonezvi: The legal and regulatory framework for the EU' shale gas exploration and production regulating public health and environmental impacts. Energ. Ecol. Environ. 2017. P 7

overdesigned to ensure safety of the operation. This first well, therefore, does not represent the optimum design and would probably cost much more than the rest of the wells that will be drilled in the field.

As this exploratory well is drilled, samples of the rock cuttings are collected and examined for their composition and fluid content. The data are used to identify the type of formation versus depth and to check on the presence of hydrocarbon materials within the rock. Cores of the formations are also obtained, preserved, and sent to specialized laboratories for analysis. Whenever a petroleum-bearing formation is drilled, the well is tested while placed on controlled production. After the well has been drilled, and sometimes at various intervals during drilling, various logs are taken. There are several logging tools or techniques (electric logs, radioactivity logs, and acoustic logs) that are used to gather information about the drilled formations. These tools are lowered into the well on a wireline (electric cable) and, as they are lowered, the measured signals are transmitted to the surface and recorded on computers. The signals collected are interpreted and produced in the form of rock and fluid properties versus depth.

The exploratory well will provide important data on rock and fluid properties, type and saturation of fluids, initial reservoir pressure, reservoir productivity, and so forth. These are essential and important data and information that are needed for the development of the field. In most situations, however, the data provided by the exploratory well will not be sufficient. Additional wells might need to be drilled to provide a better definition of the size and characteristics of the new reservoir. Of course, not every exploratory well will result in a discovery. Exploratory wells may result in hitting dry holes or they may prove the reservoir to be an uneconomical development. [1]

3. Development of Oil and Gas Fields

The success of an oil field depends on the energy available to drive oil from the reservoir rock into the wells. There are three sources of energy, but they differ enormously in effectiveness:

a) If the oil reservoir has a natural connection to water, as in an ordinary anticline, then water can displace oil out of the reservoir rock and into the wells. The efficiency of this "water drive" can drive as much as 60 percent of the original oil into the wells.

---

[1] Hussein K. Abdel-Aal Mohamed A. Aggour Mohamed A. Fahim: Petroleum and Gas Field Processing. Second Edition. Taylor & Francis Group, LLC. 2016. P 8

b) If there is initially a separate accumulation of natural gas above the oil, the operator can locate the casing perforations only in the oil-saturated zone. As the oil is produced, the gas cap expands to displace oil, but the process recovers only about 40 percent of the oil.
c) In most oil reservoirs, initially there is some natural gas dissolved in the oil. As the oil field is produced, bubbles of gas separate from the oil and push oil toward the wells. Typically, less than 20 percent of the oil is recovered. [1]

Planning the entire life of the oil field soon after the field is discovered has substantial benefits. Petroleum engineers can locate water injection wells and gas injection wells as part of the plan for drilling the early production wells. The program can be optimized for total oil recovery instead of maximizing the early cash flow. Computer simulations allow "what if" questions to be asked while planning the field.

However, simple computer simulations can be highly misleading. The computer problem is not highly difficult for a natural gas reservoir in a mythical "homogeneous isotropic" reservoir with no natural water drive. Real reservoir rocks have lots of internal structure. For instance, little streaks of mudstone a quarter

---

[1] K E N N E T H S . D E F F E Y E S: Hubbert's Peak. Princeton University Press. 2001. P 105

inch thick have a huge effect on fluid flow. The rate of flow of gas, oil, and water is highly dependent on *how much* gas, oil, and water are present. At the very birth of the modern computer age, John von Neumann identified weather forecasting and oil reservoirs as important problems requiring huge amounts of computer power. [1]

Large size could increase the probability of being discovered in several ways. We start with the idea that each oil field has a characteristic length. "Length" is just a rough concept that stands for either the width, the thickness, or the length of the oil field. Here are examples of how "length" might be involved:

a) The *volume* of an oil field depends on the "length" cubed (length times width times thickness). Oil fields with big volumes might leak enough oil to the surface to attract a crowd of drillers.
b) The *area* depends on the "length" squared (length times width). This is essentially Menard's model. The bigger the area on the map, the more likely you are to hit it when throwing a dart.
c) The *diameter* is roughly the same as "length" (length raised to the power one). An example might arise if I start my exploration drill over

---

[1] K E N N E T H S . D E F F E Y E S: Hubbert's Peak. Princeton University Press. 2001. P 106

what I think is the oil field, but if my location is wrong by more than the diameter of the oil field, it's dry hole time.

d) "Length" when raised to the zero power gives the number one.

As an example, suppose that I go to Iran and drive in a surveyor's stake at the top of each of the visible surface anticlines. On top of each stake I mark a teensy dot, a mathematical point that has neither length nor width nor thickness; the dimension of the dot is the zero power of the "length." I put the names of the anticlines on slips of paper in a hat and draw names out of the hat in random order. [1]

The very large volume of information and data collected from the various geologic and geophysical surveys and the exploratory wells are used to construct various types of maps. Contour maps are lines drawn at regular intervals of depth to show the geologic structure relative to reference points called the correlation markers. Isopach maps illustrate the variations in thickness between the correlation markers. Other important maps such as porosity maps, permeability maps, and maps showing variations in rock characteristics and structural arrangements are also produced. With all data and formation maps available, conceptual

[1] K E N N E T H S . D E F F E Y E S: Hubbert's Peak. Princeton University Press. 2001. P 114: 115

models describing the details of the structure and the location of the oil and gas within the structure are prepared.

The data available at this stage will be sufficient to estimate the petroleum reserves and decide and plan for the development of the field for commercial operation.

The development of petroleum fields involves the collective and integrated efforts and experience of many disciplines. Geologists and geophysicists are needed, to define, describe, and characterize the reservoir. Reservoir engineers set the strategy for producing the petroleum reserves and managing the reservoir for the life of the field. Production and completion engineers design the well completions and production facilities to handle the varying production methods and conditions, and drilling engineers design the well drilling programs based on well completion design. In the past, each group used to work separately and deliver its product to the next group. That is, when geologists and geophysicists finish their work, they deliver the product to the reservoir engineering group. Then, reservoir engineering would deliver the results of their work to production engineering, and so on. In almost all cases, it was necessary for each group to go back to the previous group for discussion, clarification, or request additional work. This has been realized as a very inefficient operation. In recent years, most major companies have adopted what is known as the multidisciplinary team approach for field developments. In this approach, a team consisting of engineers and scientists covering all needed disciplines is formed. The team members work together as one group throughout the field development stage. Of course, other specialists such as computer scientists, planners, cost engineers, economists, and so forth work closely with the team or may become an integral part of the team. Experience has shown that this field development approach is very efficient; more and more companies are moving in this direction.

The following sections provide brief descriptions of the roles and functions of drilling, reservoir, and production engineering. [1]

Oil and gas field development starts with the exploration activities. geological and geophysical surveys and studies are used to determine the location where a hydrocarbon reservoir may potentially exist. The results of such studies merely provide information about the potential location of the reservoir, its area, depth, and some characteristics such as faults

---

[1] Hussein K. Abdel-Aal Mohamed A. Aggour Mohamed A. Fahim: Petroleum and Gas Field Processing. Second Edition. Taylor & Francis Group, LLC. 2016. P 13: 14

and fractures. Based on the information available, a location (normally at the center of the potential reservoir) is selected to drill the first exploration well, called *wild cat*. The design of this well is based on experience since no data are yet available for proper design of the well. As this well is being drilled, rock and fluid properties data for all penetrated formations are collected and analyzed. More attention is given, and more data are collected and analyzed through the target depth of the potential reservoir. If hydrocarbons (oil and/or gas) are found, the well is tested to determine the production potential; otherwise, the well is considered a *dry well* and is abandoned.

If the wild cat is successful, more exploration wells will be drilled and tested. The number and locations of these wells are determined to provide as much information as possible about the reservoir volume, the number of hydrocarbons in place, and the production potential of the discovery. Preliminary reservoir simulation studies coupled with economic evaluations are made at this stage to determine whether the discovery is commercially viable. Once a decision is made to develop the field, extensive simulation studies will be conducted to examine various development and production strategies with the objective of determining the optimum development and production plan, which yield the maximum recovery and best economics.

Following this, well completion designs will be made with the objective of having wells work for the entire life of the field, providing maximum recovery in the most economic and safe manner. Based on the completion designs, the well drilling designs and programs will be developed. At this stage and based on the production forecast, the surface facilities for separation and treatment of produced fluids are designed. Procurement of materials and equipment is planned and made to secure their availability on time for actual field development and production.

Drilling operations then start according to schedule. Each drilled well is tested and evaluated, and the drilling program could be modified based on the data collected. To accelerate revenue, all or part of the surface production and processing facility should be on location to produce wells as they are drilled and completed.

Production data (production rates, pressures, temperatures, gas–oil ratio, and water cut, if any) are collected for a period of time and then compared against the forecasted (predicted) data from reservoir simulations. Normally, no match would be obtained. Then a process called history matching is performed where the

Petroleum Exploration

reservoir simulations are modified (by changing the data used in developing the original simulations that have the least certainty) until the simulation data match the actual production data. The modified simulations are then used to forecast future production. Again, after a period of time, the actual production data are compared against the recent simulation data. Again, no match would be obtained. The history matching process is repeated and this would probably continue until the end of the life of the field.

It should be noted that several operations, such as pressure maintenance, improved/enhanced recovery, and artificial lift, might be implemented during the production life of the field. When no more hydrocarbons can be economically produced, the field is abandoned. To do so, wells have to be killed, filled with layers of cement and sand, and the surface casing capped. This process is governed by either company or government regulations. [1]

4. Costs and planning

The amount of time needed for planning, acquiring, processing and interpreting seismic data should not be underestimated. Cycle times of 2 years from conception to final interpretation are common for 3D surveys in the

---

[1] Hussein K. Abdel-Aal Mohamed A. Aggour Mohamed A. Fahim: Petroleum and Gas Field Processing. Second Edition. Taylor & Francis Group, LLC. 2016. P 5: 6

North Sea. Although efforts are underway to improve on the time required, continued improvements in acquisition and processing technology mean that often there is an increase in cycle time and survey cost.

The cost of a seismic survey depends on the complexity of the survey, but typically varies from $10,000 (simple, marine) to $40,000 (complex, land) per square kilometer for 3D acquisition and $5000–$15,000 per square kilometer for processing. 3D surveys can be any size from 100 to 2000 square kilometers or more.

However, the determining economic factor is often the ratio to well cost. Offshore wells can be extremely expensive (North Sea wells typically cost in the order of $20 million), whereas onshore drilling is much cheaper. For this reason, large 3D surveys are often used offshore where companies are more inclined to use seismic data as a substitute for drilling at the appraisal stage. [1]

4.1. Investment in exploration

2015 marked a downturn in upstream oil investment trends, which followed an upward cycle that lasted over a decade. Investments in

---

[1]Frank Jahn, Mark Cook and Mark Graham: HYDROCARBON EXPLORATION AND PRODUCTION. 2ND EDITION. Elsevier B.V. 2008. P 46

E&P had increased six-fold since 1999, posting uninterrupted growth with the exception of 2010, when investments fell following a sharp drop in oil prices, and in 2002 when they were stagnant. Clearly, the main reason for this downturn is the drop-in oil prices since mid-2014, but it should be noted that even at the beginning of last year, many international companies were announcing strategic reorientations, favoring budgetary discipline and profitability over growth. Thus, declining oil prices have simply accelerated and amplified a shift that was already underway. This downward trend is expected to continue during 2016, albeit at a slower pace. [1]

Following a moderate 3% increase in 2014 after four years of strong growth (+60% between 2009 and 2013), investments in exploration/production (E&P) are projected to fall 21% this year to approximately $540 billion, down by more than $140 billion compared with the previous year.

This trend has been especially pronounced for independents, whose budgets fell by 34% compared with 15% for the majors, and only 11% for national companies (NOC). At the regional level, only the Middle East avoided the slump, with investments expected to rise by 3%,

---

[1] Investments in exploration/production and refining 2015. IFP Energies Nouvelles - January 2016. P 10

supported by NOCs which represent approximately 70% of regional investments. North America and Europe suffered the sharpest declines, with budgets falling by 35% and 33% respectively. The pullback in investment in Africa (-22%) and the CIS countries (-21%) was fairly close to the global average, while Asia-Oceania (¬15%) and particularly Latin America (-8%) posted smaller declines. [1]

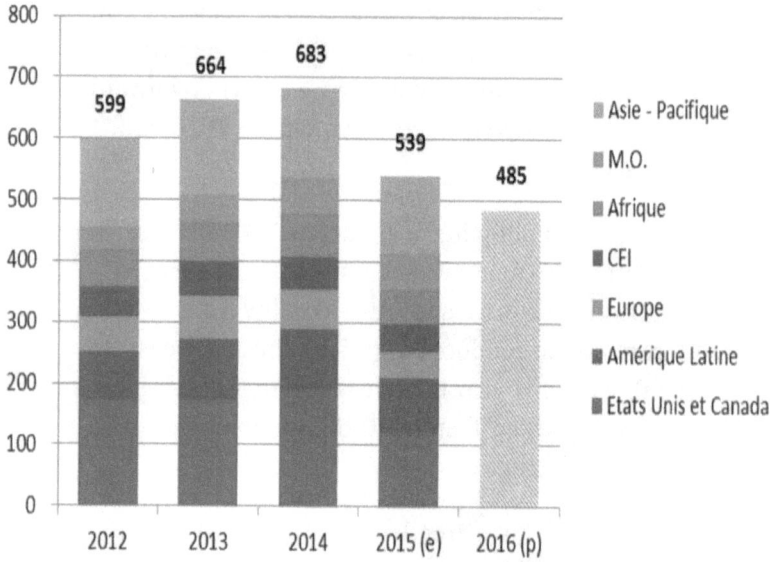

Except for the Middle East, all regions worldwide posted a net decline in investment, with relatively marked regional differences. Note that there seems to be an inverse

---

[1] Investments in exploration/production and refining 2015. IFP Energies Nouvelles - January 2016. P 10

relationship between the relative weight of NOC investments and the extent of their decline in a given region. North America and Europe, where NOCs have a small presence (aside from Statoil in Europe), suffered the largest declines, while Latin America and the Middle East - where investments by NOCs represent between 70% and 80% of the total - were less affected. The Middle East even posted moderate growth in E&P expenditures. Declines in other regions, where NOCs represent between 40% and 60% of investment (the worldwide average was 45% in 2015), fell within the middle of the range. [1]

---

[1] Investments in exploration/production and refining 2015. IFP Energies Nouvelles - January 2016. P 11

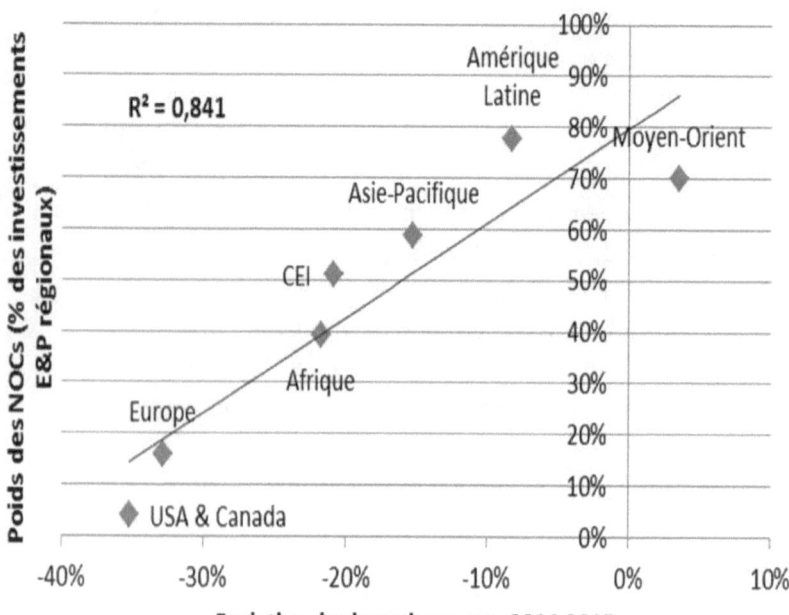

As it accelerates delivery of its 2030 strategy, Adnoc will optimize its upstream operations and drive solutions to maximize recovery from its mature reservoirs, while seeking ways to cost effectively unlock the potential of untapped resources Adnoc's key strategic investments program, according to which it plans to spend over $108.9 billion over the next five years, has received the approval of Abu Dhabi's Supreme Petroleum Council (SPC), even as the oil and gas company expands its 2030 strategy, aimed at unlocking, creating and maximizing value and ensuring smart growth in its upstream, and downstream businesses, while strengthening market access.

The SPC approved Adnoc's plans for capital expenditure of over Dh400 billion ($108.9 billion), over the next five years, as it embarks on its upstream and downstream expansion and growth projects. The SPC also approved Adnoc's plans to explore and appraise Abu Dhabi's unconventional gas resources, as the company seeks to enable future value creation from its untapped gas resources. And, the SPC gave the green light to Adnoc to pursue international downstream investments.

Dr Sultan Ahmed Al Jaber, Minister of State and Adnoc Group CEO, says: 'This marks the next phase in delivering our 2030 strategy, which will contribute to further maximizing value from all our resources, introduce new and significant partnership opportunities and enhance our capabilities to diversify our portfolio of products, as we aim to expand into key growth markets.

'In line with the SPC's directives, over the coming years, we will make strategic, commercially driven and targeted investments, across our entire value chain, aimed at maximizing existing resources, while also identifying and developing new, value-enhancing opportunities.'

He also adds: 'Furthermore, our intention to explore and appraise our unconventional resources, in collaboration with value-add, strategic partners, reinforces Adnoc's objective to further diversify our hydrocarbon assets base and enable value creation through vast untapped resources. We aim to unlock and deliver material and commercially viable production from Abu Dhabi's unconventional resources by 2030, with a focus on gas and gas liquids.'

As it accelerates delivery of its 2030 strategy, Adnoc said it continues to optimize its upstream operations and drive solutions to maximize recovery from its mature reservoirs, while seeking ways to cost effectively unlock the potential of untapped resources and leverage technology economies of scale to keep the operating cost per barrel at the most competitive level.

It remains on track to expand oil production capacity to 3.5 million barrels a day by the end of 2018, and to improve drilling time by 30 per cent by 2019. The company noted that its enhanced efficiencies have brought Adnoc's low production cost down even further, a factor driving interest in the upcoming offshore concessions, which have attracted more than 14 potential partners from across the world.

Petroleum Exploration

In gas, Adnoc is focused on ensuring a sustainable and economic supply of gas for the UAE's growing demand. To help achieve this Adnoc will access undeveloped tight reservoirs, tap into its gas caps and expand sour gas production. In addition, it has started an exploration drilling program to explore for, and appraise, the potential of individual gas deposits in tight reservoirs.

Adnoc plans to secure additional captive crude processing capacity in growth markets, establish sector specific global businesses and enhance its global marketing activities, including introducing non-speculative asset-backed trading, to further stretch the dollar from every barrel of oil it produces.

In support of its expanded 2030 strategy, Adnoc will grow its crude refining capacity by 60 per cent and more than triple its petrochemical production, to 14.4 mtpy by 2025 through a staged expansion plan aimed at initially optimizing its existing assets to grow and diversify its products portfolio. An aromatics project will convert naphtha, which is currently exported, into gasoline and aromatics and a large project to enhance the crude processing flexibility of its 900,000-bpd refining system will be taken forward.

Delivery of Adnoc's expanded 2030 strategy builds on three changes it has made to the way it operates. It has expanded its approach to partnerships, to capitalize on growth opportunities, enhanced its capital structure, to more smartly finance its business, and revised the way it manages its portfolio of assets, to drive performance and unlock lasting value.

Adnoc offered a minimum 10 per cent stake, or 1.25 billion shares, and a maximum 20 per cent stake, or 2.5 billion shares, in the partial IPO of Adnoc Distribution, its fuel distribution unit.

The Adnoc Distribution IPO, which will be the first time Adnoc has placed shares of one of its subsidiary companies onto the public markets, offers both UAE and international investors the opportunity to invest alongside Adnoc in the region's retail brand.

Meanwhile, Adnoc and Borealis, the joint venture partners in Borouge, have signed a framework agreement in which they will advance projects that will expand and add value to the downstream petrochemicals business of both companies. This comes in the context of Adnoc's expansion of its strategic partnership over its value chain as part of its 2030 growth strategy.

Adnoc and Borealis are moving to the pre-front-end engineering and design (Feed) stage for the construction of the Borouge 4 complex, which is scheduled to come on stream around 2023 and will be integrated with Adnoc's Takreer refinery. They have also commenced engineering, procurement and construction (EPC) tendering for an additional polypropylene plant (PP5) with 500,000 tpy capacity and based on Borealis's proprietary Borstar technology. PP5 will be integrated into the existing Borouge 3 complex, adding value to the surplus propylene available from Takreer's new propane dehydrogenation (PDH) unit.

Borouge's aim is to supply the automotive and energy markets as well as in pipe, agricultural film and the rigid and flexible packaging sectors. Its main target market is Asia, where polymer demand is set to double by 2040.

Adnoc's expansion plans involve bringing in new investors, including private equity in some areas, but at a holding level it will remain 100 per cent owned by the Abu Dhabi government. As such, it is assessing initial public offerings (IPOs) for some service operations.

Tightness in the gas market is leading to upward pressure on ethane costs at a time when naphtha-based production is enjoying lower costs due to lower oil prices. As the region's petrochemical industries compete with power generation and other industries over gas supply, some petrochemical producers are choosing to increase investment in naphtha-based petrochemicals production. The UAE is doing this by focusing on mixed-feed crackers.

Competition is growing among the emirates for investment in downstream industries. Abu Dhabi and Dubai are considered established petrochemicals hubs, with the former advantaged by cheaper labor and electricity costs. However, Dubai is regarded as possessing a superior port infrastructure at Jebel Ali. The other five emirates are also receiving increasing attention where cost of production is cheaper. Sharjah's Hamriyah Free Zone and the Ras al-Khaimah Free Trade Zone are seen as alternative investment destinations. Fujairah is also keen to get more downstream petrochemical investments, due to its advantage as a port city and a bunkering hub.

Rising feedstock prices, limited ethane feedstock availability, increasing construction costs and the anticipation of slower demand growth in key markets are expected to lead to a decline in the number of new project announcements. A significant risk factor for the UAE's petrochemicals industry is its current reliance on naphtha feedstock.

As well as China, Borouge is seeking to establishing sales and marketing operations in India. It has teamed up with India's Machino

Polymers, which will produce compounded polypropylene (PP) for supply to the automotive industry from PP resin sourced from Borouge.

The UAE's petrochemical developments are concentrated in Abu Dhabi, which owns the fifth largest oil reserves in the Middle East and hosts most of the olefins and polymer production capacity in the UAE. Despite the global economic downturn, Abu Dhabi continues to press ahead with plans to develop its petrochemicals industry and has made strategic acquisitions in the downward market.

In Q1 2017, Abu Dhabi completed the merger of two of its sovereign wealth funds: the International Petroleum Investment Company (IPIC), a holdings company that invests in energy and petrochemicals; and Mubadala Development Company, a vehicle for economic diversification. The new entity was named Mubadala Investment Company. Both were hit by low oil prices. The new fund has assets estimated at $130 billion. The government claims the new entity will create synergies and growth in a wide range of sectors.

Abu Dhabi is planning petrochemicals projects under the Abu Dhabi National Chemicals Company (Chemaweyaat), a JV involving Adnoc (20 per cent), IPIC (40 per cent) and the Abu Dhabi Investment Council (40 per cent), which it hopes will be the world's largest petrochemical complex, located in Khalifa Industrial Zone at Taweelah. It will include an olefins plant, aromatics complex and a range of downstream polymer and chemical units. The company's website had envisaged commercial operations in earnest in 2018, but work on the plants has stagnated in recent years, with low oil prices continuing to spell uncertainty over the future of certain high capex investments in the UAE.

It is planned that the aromatics complex will convert almost 3 mtpy of heavy and medium naphtha, supplied via pipeline from the Takreer Ruwais refinery, into paraxylene, mixed xylene and benzene. The infrastructure required to support the new complex includes a dedicated export tank farm, jetty and loading berths. The Abu Dhabi Chemicals Integration Company (Tacaamol) complex will be built at Al-Gharbia, near Adnoc's Takreer refinery at Ruwais. No completion date has been set and reports suggest it will be scaled back.

As well as China, Borouge is seeking to establishing sales and marketing operations in India. It has teamed up with India's Machino Polymers, which will produce compounded PP for supply to the automotive industry from PP resin sourced from Borouge.

Adnoc subsidiary Ruwais Fertilizer Industries (Fertil) is building a fertiliser complex with capacities of 730,000 tpy ammonia and 1.28 mtpy urea, more than doubling the company's capacities. The $1.2 billion project is facing delays due to technical problems, putting it months behind schedule. Adnoc, which owns a 66.6 per cent stake in Fertile, will supply the plant's natural gas feedstock requirements. Samsung Engineering was awarded a lump-sum turnkey contract in 2009 for the complex at Ruwais and is responsible for the EPC of the complex. [1]

US crane sales and rental and heavy lift specialist Bigge says that its customers' requirements for safely achieving schedule optimization continues to be one of the biggest drivers for business, regardless of the industry served Business in the global heavy lift sector continues to be driven primarily by the oil and gas, offshore wind power, and nuclear powerplant industries -- although infrastructure projects remain an important staple, too.

According to Gert Hendrickx, sales director, projects, at Sarens: "Our SGC range of cranes have been specifically developed in response to the changing needs of the market, namely building oil, gas or nuclear powerplants

---

[1] New strategic investments. Al Hilal Publishing and Marketing Group. 2017

and for maintenance applications in these sectors. The onshore side of the offshore wind power sector is keeping us very busy at the moment, too. This comprises loading large elements for wind farms onto boats for erection at sea."

It was the increasing size and weight of items that Sarens' customers required lifting and moving that prompted it to further develop the SGC crane range. "The first crane in the SGC range was the SGC 120. It was completed in March 2011 and had a lifting capacity of 3,200 tonnes," says Hendrickx. "Six years later, in October 2017, we launched our second crane in the series, the SGC 140, which has the same lifting capacity but at a longer radius. Now we have two more SGC cranes in development, the SGC 90 and the SGC 250, which could come to fruition as early as Q2, 2018 and Q1, 2019, respectively. You can see, we have accelerated the development of our SGC series."

The crane is currently being derigged and shipped to Kazakhstan, where it will be used on Sarens' big Tengizchevroil (TCO) project for approximately the next three years. "The crane's design has been optimized for transportation via standard sized containers," explains Hendrickx. "We had prior experience fitting the SCG 120 into containers and it has successfully been transported around the world. With the SGC 140 we have allowed a safe window of three months to move it from Ghent, Belgium to Kazakhstan."

TCO operates the Tengiz oil field in Kazakhstan and Sarens has been working on the project since 2014 and the SCG 140 will be used to offload, store, stack, and transport refinery modules to their installation points. "Using the SGC 140 on the TCO project in Kazakhstan is a big milestone for Sarens," says Hendrickx. "It is the combination of our biggest crane to date and the biggest project in our history... but there will be more. We are eager to grow, to take things to the next level."

Another company 'going big' is international heavy lift and transport contractor Mammoet. It performed its largest lift to date for Lotte Chemical's ethylene glycol project in Louisiana, USA. In late September 2017 Mammoet used the PTC 200 DS -- the largest crane in its fleet -- to lift a 107-metre-long, 1,600 tonne wash tower.

Mammoet has also completed the expansion of its site at the Port of Freeport in Texas, USA. The company says that with the Port of Freeport being in close proximity to several major job sites the expansion allows it to accommodate increased demand to bring in, store, and distribute equipment to nearby projects quickly and efficiently. The additional space also provides a subleasing opportunity for clients in a secure site with 24-7 port patrol, Mammoet says.

Mammoet reports an increasing demand for factory-to-foundation services, such as the project it has successfully completed for a fertilizer company. The agriculture fertilizer and industrial nitrogen manufacturer required the replacement of an R-101 vessel at its plant in Southern Alberta, Canada. The vessel was constructed in Austria and Mammoet transported it from there to Canada using several modes of transport including barge, ship, and rail. Once the vessel arrived in Alberta, Mammoet removed the old R-101 vessel, weighing 410 tons. It used a Liebherr LR 11350 lattice boom crawler crane. At the time it was the biggest crane available in Canada, with a boom length of 126 m and a capacity of 1,350 tons. It was needed because both the old and new vessel had to be lifted up 72 m through the roof.

Italian heavy transport and lifting service provider Fagioli has also announced the completion and near conclusion of a range of diverse projects. The company has been particularly busy in India where projects include: the lifting, skidding and lowering of a 100 ton generator; the lifting a 130 ton boiler drum in In Rourkela; and the lifting a 630 ton monolithic memorial stone in Bangalore. The stone had to be raised by two meters to rotate it.

In Fagioli's home country, Italy, it has also completed the initial phase of a load-out and load-in, sea fastening and transportation project involving eight GTG modules and seven PAUs for the oil and gas industry. The project also involved Fagioli stacking an upper main module on top of a lower main module using a combination of skidding, tower lift and strand jack systems. The upper GTG module weighed 997 tons and was 57.7 m long, 15.9 m wide, and 11.2 m high. In 2018 Fagioli will de-stack the modules and load them onto a boat at a port in Central Italy.

Fagioli is also nearing the end of its long-term Mo.s.e project. This involved transporting and installing barriers to help protect the city of Venice from flooding. For this high-profile job Fagioli developed tailor made launching gantry lifting system weighing 360 tons. It comprised four tower sections (top frames), two crosshead beams equipped with four L180 ton strand jacks designed to lift and position 19 off 210-ton mobile barriers into the water.

Finally, Fagioli has announced it has opened a new branch in Indonesia to help extend its services to this part of the world. This expansion comes following a positive spell for the company. Global heavy lift provider, ALE, has also completed of a number of high-profile projects. At the time of writing it was dismantling its AL.SK190 crane at Earls Court, London, UK where it lifted 61 portal beams, weighing between 100 and 1,500 tons for construction engineering company Keltbray. While on the job site ALE says it performed the largest single lift undertaken in UK history by a land-based crane by lifting a beam weighing 1,500 tons in just 2.5 hours in June 2017.

ALE also launched the Zezelj bridge in Novi Sad, Serbia, in October 2017. In total the bridge weighed 11,100 tons and was 474 m long. ALE was contracted by Spanish civil engineering and construction services company Azvi to perform the bridge launch. The project started in June 2017 and involved jacking as well as launching two arches and the installation of two span sections.

ALE deployed jacks, a skidding system, and three pontoons combined with hydraulic winches, a ballast system, and a bespoke gantry designed especially for the project. The first manoeuvre consisted of jacking-up the first bridge section, which weighed 4,750 tons, using 16 jacks with a 7,600 ton capacity. ALE adapted the height of the gantry for several river levels and used a modular steel structure with the combination of hydraulic jacks on top the main columns.

The second arch measured 220 m long and weighed 6,400 tons and was launched in the same way as the first. The operation took five days, spread over four-months.

ALE has boosted its heavy lift equipment portfolio with the launch of a new 1,000 ton capacity telescopic lifting gantry: the TLG1000. ALE says the four-tower lifting gantry is the first system in a new fleet of high capacity hydraulic gantries. It has a variable track width, running on tracks between 915 mm (standard) and 1,750 mm wide for greater stability. The three-stage system has a 1,000 ton capacity at all stages up to 12 m high. It also has additional safety features, including a mechanical lock system and monitoring systems to check any ground settlements or tower deflections.

"As users, we know what works in practice and we couldn't find anything else on the market which fulfilled our needs," explains ALE technical director, Ronald Hoefmans. "We wanted a lifting solution that has a high capacity without compromising on stability. This lifting gantry has been designed with more horizontal loading than other standard systems on the market. Furthermore, it is not only stronger but the lifting capacity of the system remains the same throughout all three stages of the lifting process."

The TLG1000 has been function and load tested at ALE's R&D facilities in the Netherlands and is currently being shipped to its inaugural project in South America. [1]

Africa's annual appetite for gasoil and petrol is expected to climb by as much as 8%, while demand for LPG has hit double digits. The continent's growing home-grown energy supply will help satisfy some of the burgeoning demand.

Africa produced 8.4m b/d of crude last year – 77% came from Nigeria, Algeria, Egypt and Angola, according to PricewaterhouseCoopers' (PWC) 2016 Africa Oil & Gas Review. But East Africa is elbowing its way under the spotlight and changing Africa's energy map – a move easily justified by its wealth of oil and gas assets. For example, Tanzania hopes to use its 55 trillion cubic feet of natural gas reserves to become an LNG exporter by 2025, while Tullow and Canada's Africa Oil have identified 600m barrels of oil reserves in Kenya's South Lokichar basin.

Many projects are still in the exploratory stage, but investors' appetite has

---

[1] Oil and gas drive business in the heavy lift sector. Al Hilal Publishing and Marketing Group. 2017

strengthened East Africa's position in the global energy arena.

Tanzania, Kenya and Uganda are amongst several East African countries addressing wobbly regulatory frameworks by establishing bidding rounds – a more transparent way to allocate resources. Plus, the East African Community (EAC) hopes to invest around $1.5 billion to build 1,454 kilometers of intra-regional and domestic pipelines over the next few years. The longest pipeline will be the 784-kilometer route through Kenya – Uganda – Rwanda, which should significantly bolster fuel trade between the three countries.

East Africa must react quickly to satisfy the demand of its thriving middle-class. Such households in eleven sub-Saharan African countries – including Tanzania, Kenya and Uganda – are expected to more than double from 15 million people to over 40 million by 2030, according to Standard Bank's research. The subsequent appetite for oil products is vast, with a large portion earmarked to powering personal cars on newly paved roads. Most of the LPG demand will be absorbed by cooking to support the rapidly growing populations in Africa's cities, which will also help boost the region's green credentials.

Robust growth, wherever it is, always attracts global investors' attention. The time is right to explore African assets, with additional ports now in play in Tanzania, Kenya and Mozambique. However, only the strongest players will survive in what is an increasingly competitive space.

Tanzania, Kenya and Uganda are spearheading East Africa's economic prowess, with the eastern region as a whole expected to grow by 5-8%

in 2016-2017, according to the International Monetary Fund. With many energy hubs in the Middle East and North Africa (MENA) beset by political strife, the largely stable democracies in the EAC offers investors respite; the EAC demands strong governance and human rights. Plus, lower crude prices since June 2014 have triggered a rising oversupply and pushed the market into contango. This has boosted investments in oil storage and traders that have access to physical oil and storage can significantly bolster their profit margins.

The outlook for higher future prices has become particularly striking in the last three months as the surplus of crude oil production has increased stockpiles worldwide, exceeding capacity in many trading ports and forcing traders to seek alternatives. The high rates for very large crude carriers means floating storage is still an unpopular second choice.

The changing market structure has presented a gateway for global trading and storage firms to enter and widen their footprint in new markets in Africa, building on already strong platforms in the Gulf, Asia and Europe. If the oversupply of oil persists, traders may become bolder and secure their own storage facilities. They may also need to incorporate more blending capabilities and roll out additional jetties to widen their mandates to help cater for future growth.

Governments and national oil companies are also joining the rush to Africa's east coast. Oman is looking to build a foothold to promote trade of fuel and crude into the vast landlocked interior of Africa via Oman Trading International with a $50 million investment in facilities to store fuel in Mozambique or Tanzania. [1]

The global bulk liquids storage and infrastructure industry sits in the middle of a very active merger and acquisition market and there is no sign of this slowing, given underlying business drivers and the intentions of key transaction players.

Energy is vital to the economy but an investor is largely driven by upstream 'mining'

---

[1] Tank storage magazine: Oil storage opportunities amid Africa's soaring energy demand. Volume 12, Issue 7.2017.

activities in oil and coal. However, these come with significant exploration and commodity price risks – risks that financial investors are not willing to take.

Energy transportation infrastructure is one of the most attractive areas for investors, who are looking to capitalize on the resilience of this sector without taking any risk on the underlying energy commodities, namely coal, oil and gas.

Liquid storage terminals play on the movement of the largest energy commodity – oil – as well as other bulk liquid cargoes including chemicals and bio fuels. The scale of opportunity, oil price movements and the converging interests of the players involved have resulted in multiple M&A transactions and many more will follow. To understand where the transactions are coming from and what will continue to drive them, it is important to understand each interested party's dynamics.

Historically oil storage and transmission assets have been owned by integrated oil and gas majors and downstream oil refiners. In the more recent past, driven by the need to clean up balance sheets, release capital in a declining oil price environment and downward pressure on refining margins, the oil strategies have been coming to market with assets to sell. BP coming to markets to sell its interest in the Amsterdam oil terminal is a case in point.

Vopak, the leader among independent oil terminals players, control 10% of global market share. Three others – Oil tanking, NuStar and Magellan Midstream are the only ones with any near level of global scale. The need to consolidate as an industry and the need to respond to change in global trade patterns will continue to throw transaction opportunities.

LBC Terminals is currently in the market to sell part of their European assets and Vopak, who have been an active seller of terminals in the market, are key drivers of this trend.

Almost all the major oil traders (Glencore, Gunvor, Trafigura, Vitol, Mercuria and Noble) and some regional/smaller oil traders (Bright Oil, BB Energy, Concord, Galana and Hin Leong) have invested in and run oil logistics assets including storage terminals. Ownership of logistics assets did provide superior control through the supply chain and leverage to extract margins which would otherwise get lost in the trade.
In the more recent past, traders' balance sheets have gone through severe strains resulting from commodity price declines, which limits their ability to raise capital beyond a level

without capital releases from existing assets. These factors may lead traders to come to market to monetize some of their logistics assets, especially if it can be done through sale and leaseback arrangements where operational control can be retained post sale. Glencore coming to market is a case in point and more will follow.

For infrastructure funds, oil storage and port terminal assets offer an attractive business model incorporating infrastructure characteristics that investors prefer.

Storage businesses generate the bulk of their revenues from storage fees derived from leasing space in tanks. These contracts vary in length and complexity, often depending on the client. Contracts are often take-or-pay, which means the client pays even if they don't use a tank. This provides a level of guaranteed income.

Terminal businesses charge fees for moving product from tanks to transport points – be it barges, transmission pipelines and rail or road networks. These 'through-put' fees alongside other services such as heating, mixing and blending of products provide investors with additional sources of revenues. In addition, on the back of oil storage, these enterprises have become larger liquid businesses encompassing chemicals, vegetable oils and even food additives. This 'de-risks' the business by reducing its reliance on oil-based products such as crude, aviation fuel, diesel or kerosene.

In the very recent past the oversupply of crude and the contango in the forward curve have offered handsome rewards to anyone with capacity to stash oil. These market fundamentals have spurred the immediate rush to invest in new oil storage assets or acquire existing ones.

Success in the sector in part comes from buying storage terminals in the right strategic locations. Across the globe there are four key liquid storage hubs – Houston, the ARA region, the straits of Homuraz/Fujairah and the straits of Singapore. The closer the storage facilities are to suppliers' markets or required transport networks the better. Investors' affinity for OECD markets has meant there has been greater deal activity in Europe. Going forward one can expect Australia, Singapore and Houston to catch up before we see a lot of financial investor activity in the Middle East region. The recent bid process and aggressive pricing for the sale of a minority stake in Universal Terminals in Singapore could be an early indicator of this trend. Universal Terminals is Singapore's largest independent oil storage provider, with a capacity of 2.33 million m3 across 78 tanks. The ARA region is a strong gateway for Europe – a region which has seen a lot of transaction activity. iCON Infrastructure's most recent investment, Service Terminal Rotterdam, was made in this region. Antin's Infrastructure's PISTO-owned Le Havre oil terminal on France's northwest coast, is another example of a strategic location as it is the key entry point for oil products (crude and refined) in northern France. The asset has immediate access to the TRAPIL pipeline (also partially owned by Pisto), which links the business to a number of France's major airports and cities, including Paris.

Customer base is another key concern for infrastructure investors seeking stable returns from these assets. Contract renewals are one of the major risks of the business. The more revenue locked over the long-term the better. Antin's PISTO also stores for the SAGESS – the French State's strategic oil reserve –which contributes to stable long-term revenues of the company. Macquarie's TanQuid counts the German equivalent, the EBV, as one of its customers, according to sources. Whilst it's not known what type of contracts will be available at Vopak's UK storage terminals, which it recently divested, fellow seller BP has said it would look to enter a long-term capacity agreement with a potential buyer, which should offer infrastructure investors some comfort regarding revenue security.

Storage assets are not without their operational risks. Health and safety requirements have tightened since incidents such as the Buncefield fire. Costs attached to health and safety requirements – such as the Netherland's PGS 29 legislation, which outlines how liquids can and can't be stored, have also been increasing. Owners of storage assets have little scope for passing these costs on because the assets are not generally regulated, with new requirements – now occurring on more periodic cycles – likely to eat into potential returns.

Investors have had success investing in liquid storage and transmission assets – 3i's 15.4% internal rate of return (IRR) from its investment in Oil tanking subsidiaries in Malta, Singapore and Amsterdam since 2007 – is a case in point.

The oil storage business will continue to attract infrastructure investors' attention over the next few years. By investing in these assets, infrastructure investors – whilst not taking direct commodity exposure – are indirectly taking a view on the market for the products they store. But with established customers, strategic locations and long-term contracts in place, these assets have shown that they can deliver mid-teen IRRs for investors willing to take the risk. Beyond standalone economics – investors also have an eye on building a network of these assets. This will deliver benefits of being able to deploy larger quanta of capital in high-return generating assets. Macquarie seems particularly keen on this play and is not afraid of paying rich premiums – 18x enterprise value EBITDA on the Universal Terminals transaction.

On another live transaction – the sale of the Portuguese, Spanish and French assets – Macquarie again seems to be the front runner. The successful outcome on the LBC transaction could trigger many other marginal independent storage providers to follow suit. [1]

4.2. Oil Sand Exploration

Heavy oil and bitumen (the component of interest in tar sand) are often defined (loosely and incorrectly) in terms of API gravity. A more appropriate definition of bitumen, which sets it aside from heavy oil and conventional petroleum, is based on the definition offered by the US government as the extremely viscous hydrocarbon which is not recoverable in its natural state by conventional oil well production methods including currently used enhanced recovery techniques.

By inference, conventional petroleum and heavy oil (recoverable by conventional oil well production methods including currently

---

[1]Rahul Saikia: worth the investment risk. Tank storage magazine. Volume 12, Issue 4.2016.

used enhanced recovery techniques) are different to tar sand bitumen. Be that as it may, in some stage of production, conventional petroleum (in the later stages of recovery) and heavy oil (in the earlier stages of recovery) may require the application of enhanced oil recovery methods for recovery. [1]

4.3. Existing Research on Gas Hydrates

The research on gas hydrates can be categorized based on the research subjects of the efforts and application types. In terms of the types of research subjects, the categories include: (1) basic research, which focuses on the physical properties, phase equilibrium and kinetics of gas hydrate and so on; (2) geologic explorations of natural gas hydrate resources, which focus on the geological setting, bottom simulating reflectors, geochemical anomalies around gas hydrate reservoirs and so on; (3) simulation techniques for the formation and dissociation processes, which include analytical, numerical and experimental methods; (4) hydrate-based new technologies, such as thermal energy storage, separation of gas mixtures, storage of natural gas. Alternatively, previous studies on gas hydrates can be grouped based on their application types where the advances in this topic can be followed in chronological order, i.e., (1) flow assurance; (2) energy

[1]Ripudaman Malhotra: Fossil Energy. Springer Science+Business Media New York 2013. P 42

recovery; (3) hydrate-based new technologies (gas storage/transportation); and (4) environmental applications (safety and climate change). The following context is based on the second classification method.

Interest in gas hydrates was firstly sparked in the early 19th century by chemists when making hydrates of different gases, mostly as a curiosity in the laboratory. In 1778, gas hydrates were first obtained by Priestley by means of bubbling SO_2 through 2 C water at atmosphere pressure. In 1810, Sir Humphry Davy observed that a solid could be formed when an aqueous solution of chlorine was cooled to a temperature below 9 C. Faraday confirmed the existence of this solid compound, the composition of which was believed to be 1 part of chlorine and 10 parts of water. It is now recognized that more than 100 species of gases can be combined with water to form nonstoichiometric solid compounds, to which the term "gas hydrates" has been applied. During the first 100 years after the discovery of gas hydrates, most interest in these compounds was pure academic. And the primary efforts were to understand (1) what species can form hydrates and (2) what are the thermodynamic conditions for the gas hydrates formation.

Industrial interest in gas hydrates began in the 1930s, accompanying the booming of gas and oil industry, due to the discovery that hydrate formation could plug natural gas pipelines. In 1934, Hammerschmidt noted that blockage observed in some gas-transmission pipelines was gas hydrates rather than ice. Thereafter much research including extensive thermodynamic studies was carried out to understand the conditions of hydrate formation. As commented by Phale et al, until recently, the natural gas industry considered methane hydrates only as a nuisance, which occasionally plugs up pipelines or causes wellbores to collapse. However, this promoted intense research efforts on natural gas hydrates by industry, government, and academia. More information about these research efforts can be found in the monograph of Deaton and Frost.

The third period in the history of gas hydrates studies was initiated by the discovery of naturally occurring gas hydrates under different geological formations. In the 1960s, it was realized that clathrate hydrates of natural gas exist in vast quantities in the earth's crust. For example, gas production from naturally occurring hydrate deposits was reported in the Messoyakha field in western Siberia where an interval saturated with gas hydrates overlaid a gas-saturated formation. The discovery of naturally occurring gas hydrates coincided with the peak of a global energy crisis, which pushed forward the study of gas hydrates in the 1970s.

Starting in the 1970s, the search for oil and gas extended into regions which were more difficult to explore, but where geological temperatures and pressures were suitable for the formation of natural gas hydrates. Natural gas hydrates, once considered merely as a nuisance in gas pipelines, were then examined as a long-term energy resource. A bottom simulating reflector was commonly employed to mark the base of gas hydrates in marine sediments. The large amounts of gas in hydrate form justified efforts to find economic recovery schemes. The need to understand gas hydrates together with other technological considerations motivated most of these research efforts.

Along with the investigations in gas hydrates as an energy resource, more concern regarding the influence of gas hydrates recovery or naturally dissociation on the climate change, ecosystems, and stability of gas hydrate reservoirs including wellbore safety has been expressed. For example, studies on the processes of formation and dissociation of gas hydrates in many recent studies are focused on the problems of hydrate formation in the face zones of boreholes, inside boreholes, and in pipelines. Despite the concern with the potentially detrimental effects, there have also been efforts in developing innovative technologies based on the characteristics of gas hydrates for various purposes, such as natural gas storage, hydrogen storage, thermal energy storage (; McCormack, 1990;), and separation of gas mixtures.

By reviewing the research on gas hydrates, the state of the art and the key challenges for the future advances in gas hydrates research can be summarized as follows. (1) In flow assurance research, a new approach, known as risk management is being developed to take the place of conventional methods such as thermodynamic chemical inhibitor injection due to economic and ecological concerns. (2) Various aspects for gas recovery from hydrate-bearing formation are being investigated for commercial recovery due to the huge potentials. (3) The environmental impact of naturally occurring hydrates is still mostly unknown but has been arousing increasing interest. (4) The use of hydrates to store fuel is an exciting prospect that has potential advantages over other storage materials. It should be noted that recovering gas hydrates from naturally occurring reservoirs serves as the major stimulus for various research on gas hydrates. And substantial computer simulations and laboratory experiments have been conducted while in situ explorations have just started. However, the behaviors of gas hydrate in porous media have not been completely understood. Permafrost hydrates are being considered for production tests in the USA, while efforts for marine gas hydrate are also being explored due to the huge amount of marine hydrates (by several orders of magnitude larger than that in the permafrost areas). [1]

4.4. Hydrocarbon Leads and Implication for Exploration and Production

Structural interpretation reveals that the study area has fairly high fault density (down-to-basin faults). These characteristics of Niger Delta fault trend with appreciable throw, which can serve as potential path ways for hydrocarbon migration and accumulation. Typical structural styles are those of the anticlines, which also have possibility of possessing multiple pay horizons, and they are major parts of most giant oil fields. Most of the field found in a given locality and stratigraphic interval in a particular fault block have 'equivalent' stratigraphic units within good trapping structures in adjacent block which can accommodate hydrocarbon.

Promising hydrocarbon leads were identified in the study area by interpreting the seismic volume both in cross-section and in horizon maps. These leads were identified based on a combination of criteria such as structural closure, relatively high amplitude interval and

---

[1]Congrui Jin • Gianluca Cusatis: New Frontiers in Oil and Gas Exploration. Springer International Publishing Switzerland 2016. P 52: 54

spatial location within proven hydrocarbon bearing intervals/horizons in adjacent fields.

The morphology and importance of reservoir and seal vary greatly between the system tracts. The high stand system tract contains fluvial-deltaic and shore face sands, while the high stand system tract is characterized by upward coarsening sands with shale intercalations, thus serving as the potential reservoir in the field.

The transgressive system tracts are sand deficient and contain abundant fine-grained sediments, rich in organic matter. They have potential for hydrocarbon source, seal and reservoir, however source and seal are mainly the dominant facies in transgressive system tract. The shale of the TST therefore forms the seal for the potential traps in the study area. The alternation of the LST, HST and TST sands and shale with associate structural styles therefore provide a combination of reservoir and seal rocks that are essential for hydrocarbon accumulation and entrapment. In the fields across the study, which consist of a complex crestal zones of largely synthetic fault traps, most of the hydrocarbons is trapped in fault closures below regional seals of the transgressive marine Ser-2-Cassidulina, Tor-Nonion-4, Ser-3-Dodo Shale, Tor-1-Uvigerina-8 and Tor-2 shale markers. Structural top maps of reservoirs show good amplitude response that are stratigraphically and structurally controlled. [1]

4.5. Oil Mining

Oil mining includes recovery of oil and/or heavy oil by drainage from reservoir beds to mine shafts or other openings driven into the rock or by drainage from the reservoir rock into mine openings driven outside the reservoir but connected with it by boreholes or mine wells.

Oil mining methods should be applied in reservoirs that have significant residual oil saturation and have reservoir or fluid properties that make production by conventional methods inefficient or impossible. The high well density in improved oil mining usually compensates for the inefficient production caused by reservoir heterogeneity.

However, close well spacing can also magnify the deleterious effects of reservoir heterogeneity. If a high-permeability streak exists with a lateral extent that is less than the inter-well spacing of conventional wells but is comparable to that of improved oil mining, the channeling is more unfavorable for the improved oil mining method. [2]

---

[1]Chidozie Izuchukwu Princeton Dim: Hydrocarbon Prospectivity in the Eastern Coastal Swamp Depo-belt of the Niger Delta Basin. 2017. P 64: 66

4.6. Tar Sand Mining

The bitumen occurring in tar sand deposits poses a major recovery problem. The material is notoriously immobile at formation temperatures and must therefore require some stimulation (usually by thermal means) in order to ensure recovery.

Alternately, proposals have been noted which advocate bitumen recovery by solvent flooding or by the use of emulsifiers. There is no doubt that with time, one or more of these functions may come to fruition, but for the present, the two commercial operations rely on the mining technique.

The alternative to in situ processing is to mine tar sand, transport the mined material to a processing plant, extract the bitumen, and dispose of the waste sand.

Such a procedure is often referred to as oil mining. This is the term applied to the surface or subsurface excavation of petroleum-bearing formations for subsequent removal of the heavy oil or bitumen by washing, flotation, or retorting treatments.

The tar sand mining method of recovery has received considerable attention

---

[2]Ripudaman Malhotra: Fossil Energy. Springer Science+Business Media New York 2013. P 42

since it was chosen as the technique of preference for the only two commercial bitumen recovery plants in operation in North America. In situ processes have been tested many times in the United States, Canada, and other parts of the world and are ready for commercialization. There are also conceptual schemes that are a combination of both mining (aboveground recovery) and in situ (non-mining recovery) methods. [1]

4.7. Non-mining Methods

Whereas conventional crude oils may have a viscosity of several poise (at 40 C, 105 F), the tar sand bitumen has a viscosity of the order of 50,000–1,000,000 cP or more at formation temperatures (approximately 0–10 C, 32–50 F depending upon the season). This offers a formidable (but not insurmountable) obstacle to bitumen recovery.

In principle, the non-mining recovery of bitumen from tar sand deposits is an enhanced recovery technique and requires the injection of a fluid into the formation through an injection wall. This leads to the in-situ displacement of the bitumen from the sand followed by bitumen production at the surface through an egress well (production well).

---

[1]Ripudaman Malhotra: Fossil Energy. Springer Science+Business Media New York 2013. P 42: 43

In tar sand deposits, it is often desirable to initiate enhanced oil recovery (EOR) operations as early as possible, which mean considerably abbreviating conventional secondary recovery operations or bypassing them altogether. Thermal floods using steam and controlled in situ combustion methods are also used. Thermal methods of recovery reduce the viscosity of the crude oil by heat so that it flows more easily into the production well.

The technologies applied to oil recovery involve different concepts, some of which can cause changes to the oil during production. Technologies such as alkaline flooding, microemulsion (micellar/emulsion) flooding, polymer-augmented waterflooding, and carbon dioxide miscible/immiscible flooding do not require or cause any change to the oil. The steaming technologies may cause some steam distillation that can augment the process when the steam-distilled material moves with the steam front and acts as a solvent for oil ahead of the steam front. Again, there is no change to the oil although there may be favorable compositional changes to the oil insofar as lighter fractions are recovered and heavier materials remain in the reservoir.

The technology where changes do occur involves combustion of the oil in situ. The concept of any combustion technology requires that the oil be partially combusted and that thermal decomposition occur to other parts of the oil. This is sufficient to cause irreversible chemical and physical changes to the oil to the extent that the product is markedly different to the oil-in-place, indicating upgrading of the bitumen during the process. Recognition of this phenomenon is essential before combustion technologies are applied to oil recovery.

Thermal recovery methods have found most use when heavy oil or bitumen has an extremely high viscosity under reservoir conditions.

For example, bitumen is highly viscous, with a viscosity ranging up to a million centipoises or more at the reservoir conditions. Thermal-enhanced oil recovery processes (i.e., cyclic steam injection, steam flooding, and in situ combustion) add heat to the reservoir to reduce oil viscosity and/or to vaporize the oil. In both instances, the oil is made more mobile so that it can be more effectively driven to producing wells. In addition to adding heat, these processes provide a driving force (pressure) to move oil to producing wells.

In the modified in situ extraction processes, combinations of in situ and mining techniques are used to access the reservoir. A portion of the reservoir rock must be removed to enable application of the in-situ extraction technology. The most common method is to enter the reservoir through a large-diameter vertical shaft, excavate horizontal drifts from the bottom of the shaft, and drill injection and production wells horizontally from the drifts. Thermal extraction processes are then applied through the wells. When the horizontal wells are drilled at or near the base of the tar sand reservoir, the injected heat rises from the injection wells through the reservoir, and drainage of produced fluids to the production wells is assisted by gravity.

There are, however, several serious constraints that are particularly important and relate to bulk properties of the tar sand and the bitumen. In fact, both must be considered in the context of bitumen recovery by non-mining techniques. For example, the Canadian deposits are unconsolidated sands with a porosity ranging up to about 45% whereas other deposits may range from predominantly low porosity, low-permeability consolidated sand to, in a few instances, unconsolidated sands. In addition, the bitumen properties are not conducive to fluid flow under deposit conditions. Nevertheless, where the general nature of the deposits prohibits the application of a mining technique, a non-mining method may be the only feasible bitumen recovery option.

Another general constraint to bitumen recovery by non-mining methods is the relatively low injectivity of tar sand formations. Thus, it is usually necessary to inject displacement or recovery finds at a pressure such that fracturing (parting) is achieved. Such a technique therefore changes the reservoir profile and introduces a series of channels through which fluids can flow from the injection well to the production well. On the other hand, the technique may be disadvantageous insofar as the fracture occurs along the path of least resistance, giving undesirable (i.e., inefficient) flow characteristics within the reservoir between the injection and production wells, leaving a large part of the reservoir relatively untouched by the displacement or recovery fluids.

Another general constraint to bitumen recovery by non-mining methods is the relatively low injectivity of tar sand formations. It is usually necessary to inject displacement/recovery fluids at a pressure such that fracturing (parting) is achieved.

Such a technique, therefore, changes the reservoir profile and introduces a series of channels through which fluids can flow from the injection well to the production well. On the other hand, the technique may be disadvantageous insofar as the fracture occurs along the path of least resistance giving undesirable (i.e., inefficient) flow characteristics within the reservoir between the injection and production wells which leave a part of the reservoir relatively untouched by the displacement or recovery fluids. [1]

5. Land and leasing

Exploration for hydrocarbon involves not only geology and geophysics but is vitally dependent upon acquisition of rights to drill on the prospects that are generated by the explorationists. It makes little sense to explore unless one controls the land on which to drill. Landmen work closely with explorationists to lease the lands having most promise of new production, and to do so at the earliest possible stage when lease prices are lowest.

The situation on drilling rights is much different in the United States than in other countries because the U.S. is the only hydrocarbon-producing nation that permits private ownership of mineral rights. Everywhere else, the government owns the minerals. For this reason, leasing of land with right to drill is much more competitive in the United States, and oil companies have staffs of landmen and scouts who keep close check on where leases are being bought and dropped, and by whom.[2]

---

[1] Ripudaman Malhotra: Fossil Energy. Springer Science+Business Media New York 2013. P 48: 50

A typical oil lease gives the company the right to explore and drill on the lease in exchange for a yearly leasing fee called a rental, and if production is found, the owner of the mineral rights will receive an overriding royalty on production. The company takes all the risk of exploration and production in exchange for the right to drill, and the owner gets a specified percentage of the gross value of the production from the first day on. The overriding royalty was traditionally an eighth, but now, with increased competition for promising land, may be as high as 30%. Failure to pay rental results in forfeiture of the lease. If production is found, the lease will be "held by production" for as long as there is production.

It is possible for any person or group of people or any company to lease and drill in the United States, and it is because of the free enterprise system and private ownership of minerals that wildcatting and the wildcatter are exclusively American phenomena. Private ownership has led to over 600000 wells presently producing in the United States, compared to about 100000 wells in all of the other nations in the free world, and has led to the making and breaking of many fortunes in the past 80 years or so since Spindletop. [1]

---

[2] R.L.Sengbush: petroleum exploration, a quantitative introduction, library of congress 1st edition 1986. p 65

The US Department of the Interior issued a draft proposed 2019-24 US Outer Continental Shelf oil and gas leasing program which would make more than 90% of the nation's federal offshore acreage available and schedule the largest number of lease sales there in history. The current 2017-22 program enacted late in the Obama administration put 94% of the OCS off-limits to oil and gas activity, DOI officials noted.

"Today's announcement lays out the options that are on the table and starts a lengthy and robust public comment period," US Interior Sec. Ryan Zinke said on Jan. 4 as the draft was released. "Just like mining, not all areas are appropriate for offshore drilling, and we will take that into consideration in the coming weeks."

The draft proposed program (DPP) includes 47 potential lease sales in 25 of the 26 planning areas–19 off Alaska, 7 on the Pacific OCS, 12 in the Gulf of Mexico, and 9 on the Atlantic OCS. Inclusion of an area in the DPP does not ensure it will be included in the final program or offered in a lease sale because many decision points remain, DOI officials emphasized.

---

[1] R.L.Sengbush: petroleum exploration, a quantitative introduction, library of congress 1st edition 1986. p 65

Walter D. Cruikshank, acting director at the US Bureau of Ocean Energy Management, which will oversee the program, said the 2017-22 program will be implemented until the new OCS program is approved.

Oil and gas industry association officials welcomed the announcement.

"The ability to safely and responsibly access and explore our resources in the Arctic, Atlantic, Pacific, and the Eastern Gulf of Mexico is a critical part of advancing the long-term energy security of the US," said American Petroleum Institute Upstream Director Erik Milito. "It will also encourage economic growth, spur manufacturing and investment, create thousands of additional US jobs, and strengthen our national security."

Independent Petroleum Association of America Pres. Barry Russell said: "Expanding access to additional offshore reserves allows the US to better understand where production potential exists and where capital should be invested. Although this is just the first step in a long process, today's proposal is exactly the signal industry needs to drive this work forward."

National Ocean Industries Association Pres. Randall B. Luthi hailed the start of a "truly national discussion" about US offshore energy potential.

"To kick off a national discussion, you need a national plan–something that has been lacking the past several years," he said. "President Trump started the offshore energy discussion with his executive order. This plan continues that dialogue." The April executive order to which he referred reversed the former administration's ban on Arctic oil and gas leasing and supported OCS development (OGJ Online, Apr. 28, 2017)

Karen A. Harbert, president of the US Chamber of Commerce's Global Energy Institute, called the plan "a long-term commitment to securing our energy future" and said it would "help cement America's role as an energy superpower, creating jobs and contributing to our economy."

Congressional energy leaders also applauded DOI's action.

"This proposal shows President Trump and Sec. Zinke are serious about creating jobs and making America energy-dominant," said Sen. Bill Cassidy (R-La.), a Senate Energy and Natural Resources Committee member. "Opening the Eastern Gulf of Mexico to American energy producers will create thousands of jobs in Louisiana and other Gulf

Coast states and bring billions of dollars of investment to our country."

Other federal lawmakers expressed strong opposition.

Referring to the DPP's plans for leasing in the Eastern Gulf of Mexico and off Florida's east coast, Sen. Bill Nelson (D-Fla.) called it "an assault on Florida's economy, our national security, the will of the public, and the environment. This proposal defies all common sense, and I will do everything I can to defeat it." [1]

5.1. Petroleum Agreements and Bidding

In a License Agreement the Government issues exclusive rights to an oil company to explore within a specific area. The operations are financed by the license holder who also sells all production, often paying a royalty on production, and always paying taxes on profits. Such a fiscal regime is often called a Tax and Royalty system. The Government may insist upon an obligatory level of State participation.

In a Contract Agreement, the oil company obtains the rights to an area through a contract with the Government or its

---

[1] Nick Snow : Draft leasing program offers 90% of OCS. OGJ Washington. 2018

representative NOC. Essentially the company acts as a contractor to the Government, again funding all operations. However, in this case, title to the produced hydrocarbons is retained by the Government, and the oil company is remunerated for its costs and provided a share of the profits either in cash or in kind (i.e. a share of the produced hydrocarbons). The most common form of this type of agreement is a production sharing contract (PSC), also known as a production sharing agreement (PSA).

5.2. The Invitation to Bid

The geographic area of interest is divided up into a number of blocks by a grid, which is usually orthogonal. The size of these blocks varies from country to country and even from area to area in some cases. For example, UK North Sea license blocks are 10*20 km, Norwegian blocks 20*20 km, GoM blocks 3*3 miles and Deepwater Angola blocks approximately 100*50km.

The Government will decide at its discretion what blocks it wishes to include in any bidding round, but there is often a geographic progression, from say shallow water areas into deeper water as time moves on.

Roshdy Ebrahim

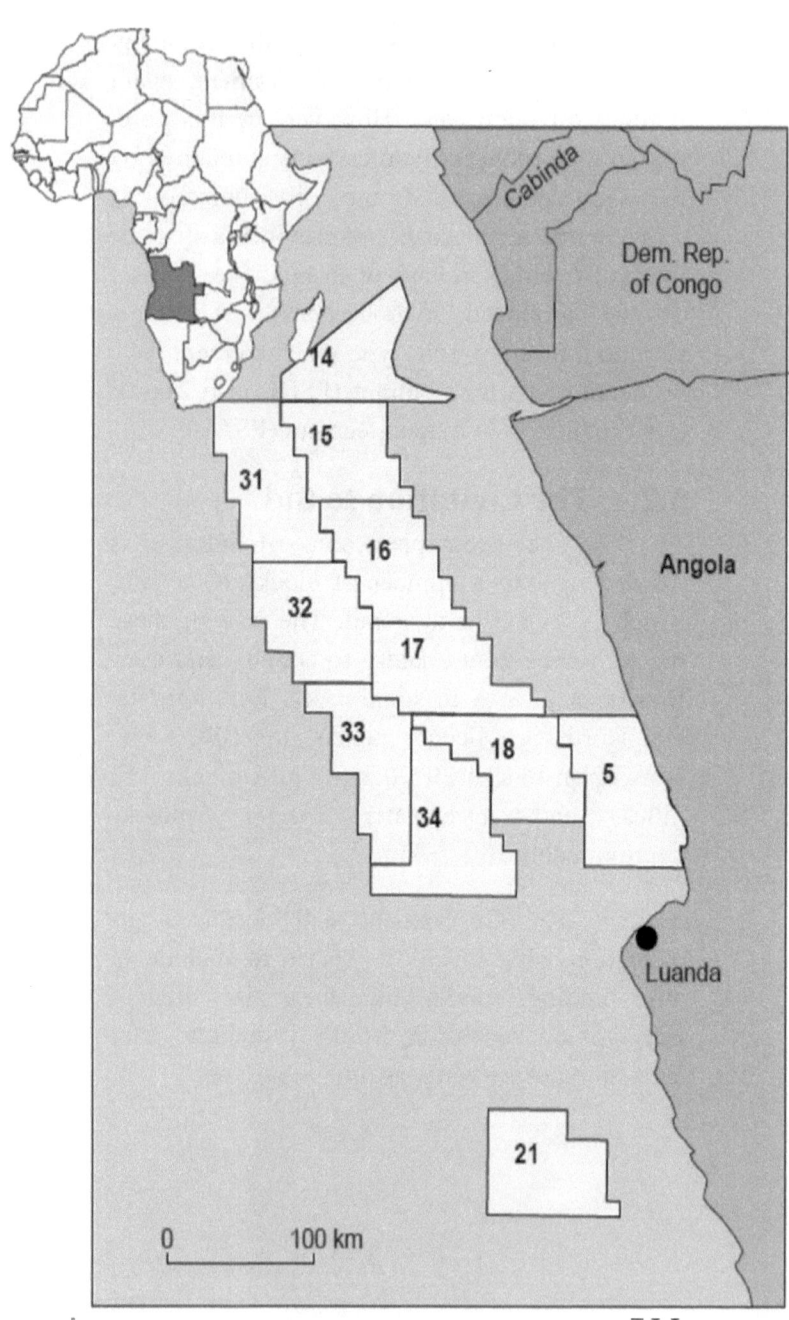

The invitation to bid may come in several forms. For example, in the UK, licensing rounds are announced periodically by the Department of Trade and Industry (DTI) on behalf of the UK Government. In 2007 the UK was offering licenses in its 24th offshore licensing round.

In any given UK licensing round, specific license blocks are offered, and an interested bidder is left to his initiative to make an evaluation of the block. This may be based on speculative regional studies performed by consultants, made available for purchase by the author, or on the company's own understanding of the block, using regional data, analogue data and any public domain information available.

The invitation to bid may not be for exploration acreage. For example, some blocks offered by Sonatrach, representing the Algerian Government, were for fields that had many years of production history. In this case, the equivalent of an information memorandum (IM) was provided to prospective bidders. This information includes both technical data for the fields, such as the production history by well, and an outline of the commercial agreement that would be expected for any participation by a foreign investor. Investors were invited to submit a forward development plan to increase the recovery of the field above the base case.

The commercial terms offer a fraction of the incremental production to the investor as the profit element of their investment. [1]

In offering an exploration opportunity in a block, the motivation of the Government is to encourage investment in form of exploration activities, such as shooting seismic and exploration drilling, with a view to development if the exploration is successful. A signature bonus may form part of the bid package. The prime objective of the oil company is to discover commercial hydrocarbons from which it can create profits by subsequent development, and it therefore considers the prospectivity of the block along with the costs of both exploration and future development.

The invitation to bid may include an outline of the form of bid required along with the fiscal terms applicable to any subsequent development. The bid may require a minimum work program consisting of seismic data to be acquired and a minimum number of wells; for example, 2000km of 2-D seismic and four wells. The bidder is of course at liberty to commit to more than the minimum, and a heavier commitment will improve the competitiveness of the bid.

---

[1] Frank Jahn, Mark Cook and Mark Graham: HYDROCARBON EXPLORATION AND PRODUCTION. 2ND EDITION. Elsevier B.V. 2008. P 9: 12

Petroleum Exploration

In many regions, especially those operating PSAs, it is normal to add a signature bonus to the work program offered. This is the promise of a cash sum payable by the successful bidder to the Government on award of the block. A minimum signature bonus may be indicated in the invitation to bid, but this element of the bid package is again a choice to be made by the bidder. In the early phases of exploration in a basin, when the risks of exploration failure are high, signature bonuses are usually tens of millions of dollars. However, once the first discoveries have been made in the area, interest will be heightened and signature bonuses offered for subsequent nearby blocks can escalate to hundreds of millions of dollars. It is important to realize that this signature bonus, once paid, is a sunk cost and should be considered as part of the cost of exploration. It is not a tax-deductible cost against future revenues.

The offer will have a bid deadline, after which submitted bids will be opened by the Government, or its NOC representative. This may be done in public or more commonly behind the closed doors. The winning bids may be publicly announced, or kept confidential, depending on the country. The criterion by which the bids are then compared is normally the total value of the bid package – the combination of the work program plus signature bonus. Of course, where the combined values of competitors are close, the Government will need to decide on the relative weighting it places on work program versus cash offered in the signature bonus. The weighting is not always apparent to the bidders. Other considerations that the Government will take into account will be the bidders' technical competence, general reputation, any existing working relationships and any strategic reasons the Government may have to encourage particular entrants into the region.

The details of the winning bids may be publicly announced and published, which is both a useful piece of information for future bids and an interesting comparison for each bidder to make with their own offer. In some cases, all bids are announced, in which case the margin by which the winner succeeded is clear – the winner of course hopes not to have outbid the next nearest competitor by an embarrassing sum, thereby 'leaving money on the table'. [1]

The successful bid will result in award of the block, giving the rights to explore.

Any signature bonus offered will be cashed by the Government. There is often a prescribed sequence of events that dictate the

---

[1] Frank Jahn, Mark Cook and Mark Graham: HYDROCARBON EXPLORATION AND PRODUCTION. 2ND EDITION. Elsevier B.V. 2008. P 12: 13

timing of carrying out the work program and declaring a commercial interest in the block – meaning that the company intends to progress beyond the exploration stage and on to appraisal and possible development of a discovery in the block. In this case, the company will need to convert the exploration rights into development rights in the block.

The figure shows an example of the provisions in a PSA for converting an exploration agreement into a production agreement.

The criteria for a commercial well would be based on production rate during testing of a discovery well, whereas the declaration of a commercial discovery (DCD) would depend on the oil company demonstrating that an economic development can be justified – this will need to pass internal economic screening criteria, the Government is due a bonus payable at DCD, and a further bonus when production from the development starts. Timeframes are typically imposed on the events, shown above for a PSA between the oil company and the Government.

In some cases, there is a requirement to release only a fraction of the block if commerciality has not been declared after a specified period of time.

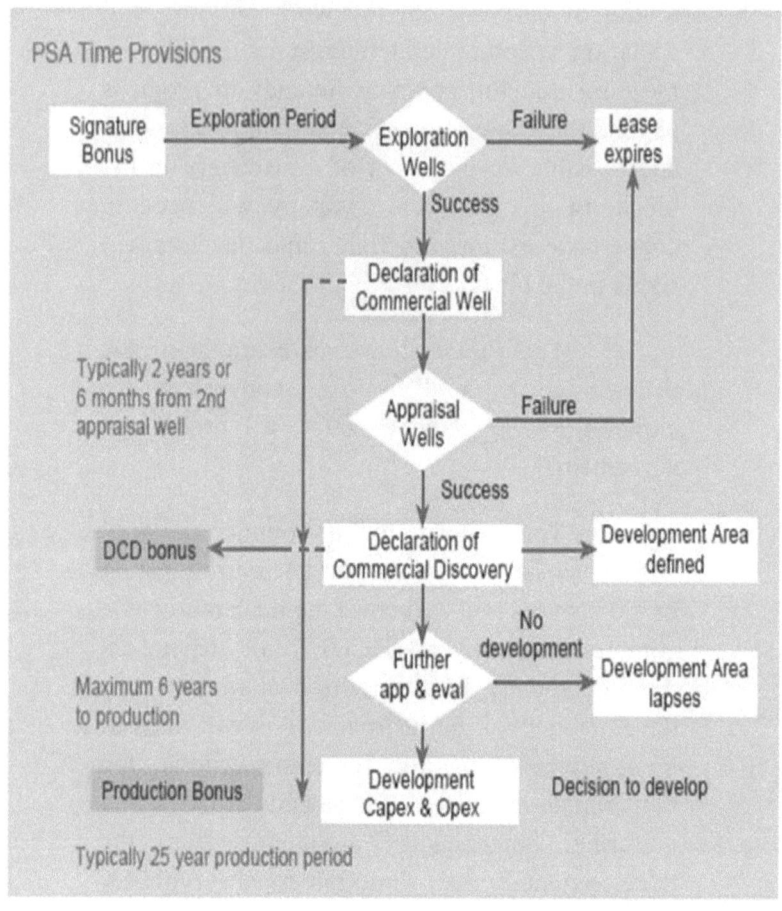

shows an example of drilling up a commitment of three wells, and shooting 2-D seismic, whilst relinquishing fractions of the block during this time. [1]

([1])Frank Jahn, Mark Cook and Mark Graham: HYDROCARBON EXPLORATION AND PRODUCTION. 2ND EDITION. Elsevier B.V. 2008. P 13: 15

5.3. The Oil Rent and General Equilibrium

For those who tend to question the fundamental basis of neoclassical theory the subject of rent still remains troubling. But what is more troubling is the message of those who stand on the fence, ideally fantasizing as if they can reconcile the differences between neoclassical theory and its *classical* counterpart by means of methodological compromises that undoubtedly promote nothing other than theoretical confusion. One such example can be seen in the treatment of oil rents by J. M. Chevalier (1976).

Chevalier starts out by defining "the oil surplus as the difference between the market price of a ton of crude oil sold to consumers in form of finished products and the total average cost incurred in discovering, producing, transporting, refining and marketing this ton of crude. At best, dealing with the notion of oil rents within the general equilibrium framework, he does not seem to realize that such a treatment tends to destroy the specificity of his rent theory at once. In addition, Chevalier maintains that due to the oligopolistic structure of oil production, and the lack of perfect mobility of capital in this industry, one has to distinguish between two types of oil rents; (1) differential rents and (2) monopoly rents (Chevalier 1976: 283–85). Of course, differential rents so defined are generated through differences in production techniques and natural qualities, whereas monopoly rents are said to be the result of the differential profit rate of oil relative to other industries. He then devises four different categories for differential oil rents: (1) quality rent, (2) position rent, (3) mining rent, and (4) technological rent. Finally, when Chevalier comes to evaluate the mechanism of price determination, he admonishes Smith, Ricardo, and Marx (and several other economists) for not being able to recognize what he alone has *discovered* about the relationship of cost and price with respect to rent—in particular on the relationship between cost and price of oil. Here is what Chevalier had to say:

> None of these economists . . . paid any attention to the determining influence of the cost trend. The price of crude oils tends to be in line with the development cost of the most expensive deposit when costs are increasing, and with the development cost of the least expensive one when costs are decreasing. Chevalier's treatment of rent is not only a mishmash of methodological misunderstanding on the meaning of rent but also a consequence of a misleading amalgamation of Marshallian cost categories and the classical and Marxian concepts of value and prices of production.

First, by abstracting from the phenomenon of property relations in the production of oil, he scarcely realizes that within the framework of general equilibrium the causative determination of the least as well as the most expensive oil deposits cannot be differentiated from each other. For general equilibrium is a framework of simultaneous determination.

Second, aside from the difficulties of a general equilibrium framework, it is not clear why the price of oil should be either in line with the cost of the least or the most productive deposits alone—given the assumption of ascending or descending cost trends respectively— and not somewhere between the two. Besides, basing the price of oil on the lowest cost deposits a priori, one cannot help but wonder about the status of higher-cost deposits and the existing differential oil rents—both empirically and theoretically. Hence a troubling ambiguity in the origin of differential oil rent at the point of production.

Here, the formulation of "quality rent," "position rent," and "mining rent" poses a formidable problem from the standpoint of identification of the origin of rent in the production process. The difference of "technical rents" from the above "rents" is also unclear.

More importantly, however, Chevalier's supposed oil rents cannot possibly assume the status of a *social category* for they are collectively devoid of any social or property relations—and without any specificity.

Hence, the choice here—other than going back to Ricardo—is between Marshall and modern general equilibrium theory. That is why Fine's narrative about the predicament of modern rent matches this occasion:

The passage to extinction of rent theory in neoclassical economics has meant that it has lived in the underworld of the profession, like a guilty conscience that is at its strongest when crime is committed but which fades with the passage of time only to reemerge sporadically and feebly.

What is also disturbing is the contagious influence of the neoclassical theory of competition (and likewise its theory of monopoly) on the remaining contemporary schools of economic thought, especially the ones that are seemingly opposed to the mainstream economic orthodoxy . As we have demonstrated, the general equilibrium approaches to the determination of "factor incomes" place all factors on the same footing, thus treating all factor incomes as rents. The difficulty of this method will be compounded further when allowing for the realization of these rents in conjunction with market structures other than "pure competition". As can be seen, Chevalier has failed to develop a *specific* theory of oil rent even within his own framework.

The next step is to show that one cannot develop a viable theory of rent for the oil industry independent of the possible impact of the ownership of oil reserves and the condition of oil leases on the accumulation of capital in the oil industry.

In this connection, we have chosen to deal with Fitch's treatment of oil rent. Even though Fitch correctly points out the shortcoming of neoclassical theory in dealing with such practical problems as the oil crisis of the early 1970s, he nevertheless fails to make a distinction between the nature of rent in classical political economy and its counterpart in Marx.

We have seen that Ricardo developed his theory of differential rent based on the differences in productivity that existed between lands of marginal and intramarginal qualities. Moreover, he maintained that the price of corn is always determined by production on marginal land, or land of inferior quality. Hence, Ricardian rent is price-determined rather than price-determining.

Unlike Marx, Ricardo rejects the notion of absolute rent and with it the impact of landed property on production in agriculture. Instead, his primary concern was the distribution of surplus among the social classes (for specific analysis see Fine 1979). Therefore, Ricardo's theory of rent, being formed at the margin of cultivation, is independent of the structure of landed property in agriculture. Moreover, Ricardo's rent theory is not consistent with his labor-embodied value theory. Striving for *specificity,* Ricardo's rent can be conceptualized either in a one-commodity world or in a multicommodity world with the prices of other goods remaining constant.

Although Fitch is critical of the prevailing view of his time, he travels on the Ricardian road to the Ricardian no destination. The veneer of Ricardo's rent theory and its semblance to that of Marx's is rather deceptive. Fitch fails, alas, to differentiate between the two very different notions of rent—the classical and the Marxian. He maintains:

By contrast, the Classical/Marxian theory accounts for the price of Persian Gulf oil without any recourse to such *dues ex machina.* The cost of production is properly understood as *unequal* for all producers and the market price is regulated by the producers operating on the basis of the least favorable conditions who are able to clear the market at a market price equal to their marginal price of production. So the result here is that surplus profits tend to originate more in primary commodities than in manufactured commodities because the range of cost differential is greater.

Clearly, the above passage departs from Marx's method of analysis and his treatment of rent in agriculture. As we have demonstrated, contrary to the *margin of cultivation thesis*, Marx argues that any one-sided movement from better to worse land is only a special case in agriculture (Marx 1981, Part VI). Even though Ricardo's treatment of rent is specific, it is valid only within a partial equilibrium framework. One has to remember that the concept of "the margin of cultivation" in Ricardian theory had been made more general by the emerging Marginalist school, for the calculation of factor incomes, before its eventual replacement by general equilibrium.

Methodologically, given the lack of consideration of the effects of landed property on the pattern of capital investment in agriculture, the Ricardian theory is caught in a dilemma of its own making: on the one hand, it loses its *specificity* if it departs from partial equilibrium; on the other hand, it remains static, restrictive, and unrealistic if it does not. Theoretically, the above theory remains ahistorical and depends on axiomatic treatment, as it fails to account for the institution of landed property and its mutual relation with the pattern of capital investments. [1]

5.4. Theory of Oil Rent and Ownership of the Oil Reserves

The phenomenon of economic rent as a category distinguished from normal profits is neither original to Marx nor specific to classical political economy. However, what made Marx's theory of agricultural rent different from his predecessors' theories is "the *specificity* of the analysis itself, not the category" (Shaikh 1981). The notion of oil rent in the oil industry is none other than the phenomenal form of the specific property relation that is unique to the oil industry.

Historically, the *separation* of the ownership of hydrocarbon deposits from the ownership of the oil fields resulted in the emergence of this barrier within the accumulation process in the production of oil. In countries or regions where the ownership of the surface soil legally includes the subsoil, the owners of particular oil leases, that is, capitalist producers, are confronted with the obstacle of ownership of the oil deposits. This relationship remains the same even if the state as a legal institutional form of landed property owns the oil lands; owing to the establishment of capitalist

[1] Cyrus Bina: A Prelude to the Foundation of Political Economy. PALGRAVE MACMILLAN. 2013. P 61:64

institutions. The separation of ownership is part of a historical process that is realized legally through the act of lease contracts, concessions, etc. At the same time, theoretically, capital investments made by the owners of the subsoil are also subsumed under the separation of ownership of the subsoil from ownership of land. The owner of the land comes to appropriate rent, while the capitalist investor tends to appropriate normal profit.

It is critical to note that the oil concessions in the Middle East and elsewhere in the world had been formed and framed to span nearly some 60 years of duration—a lengthy lease, nevertheless. These leases were signed into de facto contracts that for whatever reason renewed from time to time. In fact, there had been frequent modifications and adjustments in these concessions. For example, the revision of the original D'Arcy concession (1901) and adaption of a modified version in the 1933 concession between the Iranian government and Anglo- Iranian Oil Company (AIOC) is a case in point. Hence there are simply no "ifs" and/or "buts" in the issue of who owns oil reserves in the ground. Yet, Daniel Yergin believes that "the concessionaires" (i.e., leaseholders within the IPC) owned the reserves. We read:

One of the legacies of Mossadegh, nationalization, gave the Shah comparative flexibility [concerning the 1957 partnership with Ente Nazionale Idrocarburi]. In the other oil-producing countries, the concessionaires—the foreign companies—still owned the reserves in the ground. (1991: 504) This above statement is untrue, given that: (1) such *leases* never assumed to be equal to ownership of the oil-in-place even for the IPC itself; (2) the seeming "flexibility" of the Shah of Iran had little to do with the aborted nationalization of oil in Iran and more to do with pockets of potential oil reserves unconnected with the 1954 Iranian Oil Consortium (IOC); (3) the nationalization of oil by Mossadegh was annulled by the 1953 CIA coup d'état and de facto provisions of the IOC; and (4) Mossadegh's legacy hinges on the ownership of the sovereign, which was also acknowledged as a right of self-determination by the UN General Assembly. The last point is not only warranted but also has legal precedent in international practice.

That is why the present writer recommended the recent renationalization of oil in Argentina. Yet, Yergin keeps repeating the same nonsense:

In all the member countries, with the exception of Iran, the oil reserves in the ground actually belonged by contract to the concessionaires, the companies, thus limiting the countries control. (1991: 523) Yergin does not appreciate the difference between the *de facto* control of oil and *legal* ownership of oil reserves (oil-in-place) with respect to these concessions. He appears to take writing-off of oil royalties (as income tax) and writing-in of oil reserves (as an asset)—an ad hoc scheme by the IPC—on their face value.

A study that was completed in the early 1970s concluded that there is a major distortion in the exploration of oil that primarily "results from a widely divided ownership of land in the United States" (Miller 1973: 415). This situation stems from the fact that the oil fields are often larger than the corresponding US oil leases that belong to the firm that made the discovery. The result is that the full benefits will rarely go to the primary discoverer. To substantiate this point, Miller goes into a long discussion of the extent of *fragmentation* of oil leases through the examination of portions of profits received by the main discoverer of the field. As a first approximation, he uses the production share of the largest producer of a field as the proxy of the firm's profit share. From this empirical work, it was discovered that "the percentage of the benefits from a well-received by the discoverer declines with the size of the field" (Miller 1973: 416). Consequently, the barrier of *fragmentation* of the pattern of land ownership tends to move the capitalist investors away from engagement in new and larger oil fields that often require the assembling of large tracts of land prior to exploration. The above study also demonstrates that the "Fields under 500 acres accounted for 60.73 per cent of the [oil] fields but for only 14.43 per cent of the total area. It is again clear that most oil must lie in fields [that extend beyond] more than one ownership".

Another problem is the fragmentation of oil leases in connection with secondary and tertiary recovery methods, where the whole field needs to be put under the control of a single management, to eliminate waste and enhance the productivity of the extraction process.

This is called unitization. It would seem obvious that having a number of leases in a particular oil field undoubtedly works against production according to a predetermined schedule.

The above condition demonstrates why the firms either move toward intensive exploration in the same areas, or simply concentrate on investing in the *existing* oil fields for further recovery. Even in the case of government-owned lands, due to the existence of noncompetitive leases (and at times the practice of granting inadequately sized leases to individuals through a system of lottery) there is a great deal of speculative activity combined with a considerable fragmentation of ownership in the US oil fields.

Faced with these obstructions, capital investment is made on exploration activity within the aged US oil fields or aimed at further development of oil from existing oil wells or canalized toward foreign oil fields. The comparison of the oil-well abandonment rate in the United States, during the periods of 1965–71 and 1971–74, reveals that there has been a tremendous decline in the rate of the abandonment of commercially exhausted oil wells in the latter period, even though the average life span of oil wells declined, from 26 to 24 years, respectively (see Bina 1985: 83, Table 20). This shows that although the average life span of producing wells during the period leading up to the oil crisis (1973) was shorter than that of the crisis period, the oil wells were not abandoned as quickly as they used to be. This condition indicates, that in the United States oil was largely produced through the *successive* investments of capital upon the already-producing US oil fields. However, it was not until the early 1970s that the US oil industry experienced a substantial decline in productivity, in terms of the average oil recovery per well, as these investments were further intensified. This can also be shown from the increase in the amount of development capital expenditures (per barrel), that is, those investments that are made upon the older US oil fields, during the periods of 1966–70 and 1971–74: an increase of 7 percent as opposed to a 261 percent increase, for the period leading up to the crisis. Meanwhile, the investment in the realm of oil exploration shows an increase of about 8 percent during the period of 1971–74.

The intensification of capital investments within the existing oil fields is by and large the consequence of the impediment of the prevailing pattern of land and lease ownership in US oil production. In this context, the structure of landed property and the fragmentation of oil leases played an influential role in the direction of capital investments and the structure of accumulation in the US oil industry, long before the oil crisis of 1973–74, that set a new basis for the formation of market values, rents, and market prices at the global level. We have demonstrated elsewhere that, within the global context, the prices of all other sources of energy, including coal, natural gas, etc. are *regulated* by the *value* of oil produced from the aged US oil fields.

Given the above property relations, the formation of social value involves a process of intraindustry competition. Depending upon the extent of differential productivity, there will be value transfers from one individual capital (individual production unit) to another that would manifest themselves as differential rent. The internationalization of oil production is the manifestation of this process at the global level. During the early period in the oil industry in the Middle East and elsewhere, essentially outside the geographical boundaries of the United States, the production of oil was through the colonial contracts and in the parlance of political economy originated in rudimentary introduction of capitalism and thus *formal* subsumption of labor. However, as the material foundation of capitalism in these social formations and also within the international oil industry has further developed, the production of oil had gradually assumed the characteristic of the *real* subsumption of labor under capital at the global level. In consequence, a social *value* at the global level has emerged that systematically intertwined with the formation of differential oil rents through global competition. Based on the analysis of the previous sections, the same distinction should be made between the Ricardian (and neo-Ricardian) notion of value for the so-called marginal oil producer, and the market value grounded upon the *regulating capital* in the Marxian framework. It is not always the case that market value coincides with marginal producer in the customary norm of today. Therefore, from the theoretical standpoint, it may not be difficult to appreciate why general application of Ricardo's specific "margin," prevalent in today's mainstream theory, is not a fruitful method in the analysis of petroleum or possibly any other industries.

At the empirical level, we were able to identify the US oil fields (lower 48 states) as the least productive region of the world. The US oil fields are also the most explored oil region of the globe. Since the effect of differential oil rent of DR I cannot be separated from differential rent of the DR II, determination of the least productive oil region, in connection with the identification of the normal size of capital investment, is an impossible statistical task. We have encountered the very same problem that Marx faced a little over a century ago in agriculture. Following Marx's method, we were able to identify the specific oil fields upon which the social value of the oil was formed. Due to the integration of oil production at the global level and the fact that US oil comes from the least productive oil fields, the social value associated with the above oil fields has become the social value of the entire international oil industry. Thus, it is through the decline in the productivity of the old US oil fields located in the lower 48 states (in the 1970s), that the magnitude of the newly formed social value has been restructured simultaneously with the reorganization of the entire oil industry through the *crisis*. [1]

[1] Cyrus Bina: A Prelude to the Foundation of Political Economy. PALGRAVE MACMILLAN. 2013. P 64: 69

5.5. The Regime of the 50-50 Profit-Sharing

In the late 1940s and the early 1950s, there was a marked change in the political and economic conditions of most Third World countries.

There were some fundamental transformations in the entire world economy, which set the stage for the beginning of a new era.

In this postwar period, significant changes were also apparent in the international oil industry, and the nature and terms of oil contracts, which had already been the subject of a vigorous nationalization in Mexico (1938), and which were facing similar attempts in Iran (1951) and, much later, in Iraq (1968-72) (for Iran's case, see Elwell-Sutton 1955, Walden 1962). The significant characteristics of this period (1950-72) were the transition and transformation of the entire industry from the status of a cartel-like economic entity based on the administered pricing decisions, demand management, and the supply manipulation, to a world industry with an emerging unified competitive market, and prices that were subject to the regulation of a more developed form of capitalism on the world scale. As expected, in periods of transition such as this, one may find an assortment of fading elements of the old along with the embryonic but, nevertheless, developing constituents of the new. Some of the more distinct characteristics of this period were: the existence of long-term contracts, the establishment of the Persian Gulf basing-point system and subsequent designation of lower posted prices for its oil, the utilization of posted prices for the calculation of oil royalties and rent, and the formation of OPEC.

In this period, the control of oil was founded upon a double basing-point system, one associated with the cost of production of oil at the Gulf of Mexico and another based upon the cost of oil in the Persian Gulf (see Clark 1938, Smithies 1949, Keysen 1949, Stocking 1950, Machlup 1949). It is true that, initially, the IPC engaged in posting one "price" for both these oil-producing regions. But, as the Persian Gulf oil entered the markets in the Western Hemisphere and tended to displace US oil, the IPC was obliged to cut the posted prices, thereby admitting openly, but indirectly, an enormous margin of profitability in the IPC's Middle East operations. Paradoxically, however, cuts in the Persian Gulf basing-point posted prices led to an accelerated displacement of Western oil by its Middle Eastern counterpart.

During this period, the long-term colonial contracts had remained intact. And there was neither a spot market, nor, for that matter, a futures market in crude oil (Prast and Lax 1983). Contrary to the previous period, the calculation of the oil royalties/rents in this period was based upon posted prices rather than a fixed sum of money per barrel of oil. Therefore, the magnitude of oil royalties/rents was calibrated according to the variability of posted prices, which is theoretically a tangible step toward a *price-determined* economic rent in the oil industry. As we shall see below, with further transformation of the industry since 1974, given the emerging global spot markets and globalization of the oil industry, *posted* prices became fully dependent on the magnitude of *competitive* prices in the market, and so as the oil rents.

Finally, only after the establishment of the regime of "50–50 profit sharing," which was directly dependent on posted prices (a mechanism of appropriation of the oil rents), did the oil-exporting rentier states become interested in the magnitude of the posted prices. The higher the posted price, the larger the amount of oil rent due to be appropriated by the oil-exporting nations, OPEC and non-OPEC alike. As we have already pointed out, the formation of OPEC prompted by a unilateral reduction of the posted price in the Persian Gulf oil region. This reduction led to a steep decline in the magnitude of oil royalty collected by the oil-exporting countries in the region. Similarly, there was a simultaneous reduction in the posted price of Venezuelan oil. And this was a trigger behind the joint protest by Venezuela and the other four Persian Gulf oil producers manifested in the first meeting of OPEC in the fateful September of 1960. [1]

5.6. Contractual regimes: basic characteristics

During the second half of the twentieth century, and with the political developments round the world, the concessionary regime came to be regarded as incompatible with government sovereignty. Contractual regimes emerged as the result of efforts to modify the nature of the relationships between IOCs and host governments, and above all to find an alternative to the concessionary regime, allowing the host government, in theory, to exercise more control over both petroleum operations and the ownership of production.

Two types of contractual regimes apply: production sharing contracts (PSCs) and risk service contracts. The concept of the PSC was used firstly as early as the 1950s. But in their currently used form, PSCs in particular became popular in Indonesia in the 1960s. Risk service contracts first came into use in the late 1960s.

―――――――――――――――
[1] Cyrus Bina: A Prelude to the Foundation of Political Economy. PALGRAVE MACMILLAN. 2013. P 89: 91

Under the typical contractual systems, the oil company is appointed by the government as a contractor for operations on a certain area. The title to the hydrocarbons remains with the state, and all production belongs to the government unless it is explicitly shared, while the IOC executes petroleum operations in accordance with the terms of the contract and operates at its own risk and expense under the control of the government. The IOC also provides all the financing and technology required for the operation.

The two parties agree that the contractor will meet the exploration and development costs in return for a share of production or a cash fee for this service if production is successful.

• If the company receives a share of production (after the deduction of Government share), the system is known as a PSC – also known as a production sharing agreement (PSA) – which is a binding commercial contract between an investor – the IOC – and a state (or national oil company). A PSC defines the conditions for the exploration and development of natural resources from a specific area over a designated period of time. Under a PSC, as the company is rewarded in physical barrels, it therefore takes title to that share of petroleum extracted at the delivery point (export point from the contract area).

• If the IOC is paid a fee (often subject to taxes) for conducting production operations, the system is known as a service contract, also called a risk service contract. The latter is so called because the host government (or its national oil company) hires the services of an international oil company and, in the case of commercial production from the contractual area, the oil company is paid in cash for its services without taking title to any petroleum extracted. A distinction is sometimes made between service contracts and risk service contracts. The former is simply based on defined compensation for a specific task, while the latter may involve additional risk being taken by the contractor for which a variable fee may be applicable.

While some service contracts are disguised PSCs, especially with regard to ownership of the resource, the main differences between the two contract forms are the remuneration of the contractor and the control over operations. [1]

---

[1] Philip Daniel, Michael Keen and Charles McPherson: The Taxation of Petroleum and Minerals. international Monetary Fund. 2010. P 98: 99

5.7. Production sharing contract

Over time PSCs have changed substantially, and they now take many different forms. One cannot refer, for instance, to a typical Asian or a typical Eastern European contract. Terms vary between one country and the other. But in its most basic form a PSC has four main properties. The IOC pays a royalty on gross production to the government, if applicable. After the royalty is deducted, the IOC is entitled to a predetermined share of production for cost recovery. The remainder of the production, so called profit oil, is then shared between government and IOC at a prespecified share. The contractor then has to pay income tax on its share of profit and cost oil combined, after deductions permitted under tax law. A few systems (Angola, Russia) have used profit oil alone as the base for income tax.

In contractual regimes (as with concessionary systems), the oil company bears all the costs and risks of exploration and development. It has no right to be paid in the event that discovery and development do not occur. However, if there is a discovery the company is allowed to recover the costs it has incurred, and this is known as cost recovery or cost oil. The investor typically may take oil for cost recovery up to a fixed proportion of total production from the project, known as the cost oil limit, as compensation for the cost of exploration and development. The oil that remains after the oil company has taken its cost oil is usually termed profit oil.

Cost recovery is similar in concept to deductible expenses for tax purposes (including depreciation of capital assets) under the concessionary systems. It includes mainly unrecovered costs carried over from previous years, operating expenditures, capital expenditures, abandonment costs and some investment incentives. Financing cost or interest expense is generally not a recoverable cost, though unrecovered costs can often be rolled forward with an uplift in lieu of interest. Normally, a predetermined percentage of production is allocated on a yearly basis for cost recovery. However, in general there is a limit for cost recovery that typically ranges from 30 to 60 per cent of gross revenue, in other words, for any given period the maximum level of costs recovered is 60 per cent of revenue, although contracts with unlimited cost recovery are also in existence (see Indonesia, Bahrain and Algeria for instance). A fixed ceiling on cost oil ensures a minimum quantity of profit oil from which the state can secure up-front revenues as soon as production commences.

Many PSCs specify annual cost oil allowances either on a sliding scale or state that this variable is biddable or negotiable up to a certain maximum value.

Full cost recovery occasionally comes with a time limit attached to it. The share of production set aside for cost oil may decline after, for instance, five years, in which case it works similarly to accelerated depreciation. Unrecovered costs in any year are sometimes but not generally carried forward with interest to subsequent years. Investment incentives (credits, uplift or allowances) may also be provided to allow the contractor to recover an additional percentage of capital costs through cost recovery. The more generous the cost recovery limit is, the longer it takes for the government to realize its take. There is usually a ring fence for cost recovery around the contract area or development area – costs associated with a particular block or license must be recovered from revenues generated within that block or license.

Royalties can also feature in PSC regimes but the same economic impact can be secured by having cost oil limits below 100 per cent, together with a minimum state profit oil share, which also ensure an early flow of revenues to the state.

The principle of cost recovery applies to both a PSC and in risk-service agreements.

However, the basis of the contractor's remuneration after it has recovered its cost differs in type.

In a PSC, profit oil is divided between the host government and the company according to a pre-determined percentage negotiated in the contract. The split can be constant, or on a scale linked to cumulative or daily production rates, or there can be a progressive split linked to achieved project profitability, that is to rate of return (ROR) or R-factors.

Under ROR systems, the effective government take increases as the project ROR increases. The government is guaranteed early revenues through the operation of the cost oil ceiling which ensures there is always a minimum quantity of profit oil to be shared between the investor and the state in each year. The elements determining the R-factor, or payback ratio, vary from one country to the other, but normally both revenue and cost (and in some cases interest) are included in the equation. The R-factor can be broadly defined as the ratio of cumulative net earnings (some countries use gross revenues) to cumulative total expenditures. The R-factor is calculated in each accounting period and once a threshold is reached, a new sharing rate will apply in the next accounting period. The objective of the ROR and R-factor is to link the sharing between the government and the contractor to profitability. Over time these parameters will increase the government share of profit oil. However, in exceptional circumstances, if the ROR fell then this could lead to a fall in government's share of profit oil, but this would require a period of negative cash flows. It is theoretically possible for a substantial enhanced oil recovery (EOR) project to benefit from these circumstances if its associated investment is sufficiently large to generate negative cash flows for long enough for the ROR to fall period of negative cash flows later in the life of the field would normally result in the field ceasing production.

The contractor's share of profit oil is usually, but not always, taxable. In many PSCs the government pays the contractor's income tax from its share of profit oil; these are called 'pay on behalf' PSCs. The precise legal provisions that give effect to these 'pay on behalf' regimes are important in the context of assessing the foreign tax credit position of IOCs which may give rise to additional tax liability in their home country if poorly constructed.

In some countries, the government has the option to purchase a certain portion of the contractor's share of production at a price lower than the market price: a provision known as the domestic market obligation (DMO). There can also be additional government take in form of bonus payments, whether signature bonus or production bonus. Most tax regimes allow for bonuses to be tax deductible, since they are a cost of doing business; the larger the tax relief for the bonuses offered in the contract, the greater the magnitude of the upfront bonus is likely to be. However, they are typically not allowable for cost recovery under PSC rules, which ensures that the state receives more profit oil. [1]

5.8. Risk service contracts

In the case of service contracts, the contractor carries out development work on behalf of the host country for a fee, although in exceptional circumstances the remuneration can itself be in the form of oil. The government allows the contractor to recover the costs associated with development of the hydrocarbon resources. The government pays the contractor a fee which is agreed up-front, and remuneration under a service contract is also usually determined using project performance indicators linked to actual production rates and based on pre-agreed capital budgets. All production belongs to the government. Since the contractor does not, strictly speaking, receive a share of production, terms such as production sharing and profit oil are not appropriate, even though

[1] Philip Daniel, Michael Keen and Charles McPherson: The Taxation of Petroleum and Minerals. international Monetary Fund. 2010. P 99: 101

the arithmetic will often carve out a share of revenue in the same fashion that a PSC shares production. The fixed fee remuneration – service fee – of the contractor can be subject to tax. It is analogous to taxable income in a concessionary system and profit oil in a PSC. The service contracts are also known as risk service contracts or risk contracts: the term risk is added because the oil company puts up all the capital and risks being exposed to cost overruns which, typically, it is unable to recover.

Over time, service contracts have taken many forms; technical assistance contracts and buyback are two variations. [1]

5.9. Risk sharing

Risk is present at all stages of an oil and gas project's life cycle. It can be geological (uncertainties with respect to structure and reservoir characteristics), exploratory (chance of failure), technical (reserves and cost estimation), economic (oil and gas prices), commercial (contractual, including third-party relationships) or political (regulatory and fiscal). Risk is not only limited to the exploration phase; 'only when the deposit is exhausted do you know precisely what the reserves were.

---

[1] Philip Daniel, Michael Keen and Charles McPherson: The Taxation of Petroleum and Minerals. international Monetary Fund. 2010. P 102: 103

There is no doubt that companies have the means to diversify certain levels of risks through, for instance, a large, worldwide portfolio, but every project has to offer the prospect of acceptable risked returns that cover the cost of capital.

Given the wide range of countries that IOCs operate in and the equally diverse range of fiscal regimes that they find acceptable, investors have learnt to be pragmatic in terms of the fiscal burden they find acceptable. They naturally seek to secure the best terms they can, but this is a function of the competitive landscape and the opportunity cost of investing in better projects elsewhere. Strategic preferences differ from company to company and it certainly serves the interests of host governments to invite as many players as possible into a basin. A project that offers unacceptable returns to one company may well be acceptable to another. A regulatory framework that induces some investors to divest of assets with little activity also ensures that other companies who wish to invest have access to the opportunities and are not frustrated by unwilling investors.

The appetite of the investor depends not only on the level of tax, but also on the extent to which the government shares the project's risks. A popular construct is that in most fiscal regimes, be they a PSC or tax and royalty, with high levels of government take, the state is sharing in the project risk, by virtue of the fact that the investor gets a large tax deduction for his investment. In Norway, the marginal tax rate is 78 per cent. Therefore, if the investor invests US $100, then he gets a tax deduction of US $78, reducing his net exposure to US $22.

However, if the argument is taken to its logical conclusion then regimes with government take approaching 100 per cent should be the most attractive in eliminating risk as in these circumstances the state takes by implication nearly all the risk. In reality, the state permits relief for capital costs incurred but these are only of value if there is taxable income to relieve them against. Besides, in many cases it takes a number of years to secure the relief due to extended depreciation rules. For first-time investors, there will be no possibility of tax relief until the project commences production and generates taxable income. In these circumstances, all the exploration risk is borne by the investor: if there is no commercial discovery then the government will have taken no risk as the investor will have no income to shelter the expenditure. In contrast, if there is existing production from other projects then it will be possible to secure tax relief from failed exploration and development expenditure, assuming no ring-fencing.

Countries like Norway have gone one step further and specifically reimburse tax relief (at a rate of 78 per cent) to all investors who are not in a tax paying position.

Under a PSC, the contract is signed (and signature bonuses paid) before the IOC has had the opportunity to explore the oilfield on offer. Only when oil is discovered and successfully developed can the IOC recover its exploration expenditures. Meanwhile, financial circumstances might change; borrowing can become costlier and prices can fall. That is why the IOC has a strong incentive to accelerate the exploration and development phases to secure an early return on up-front capital. The same is also true under a tax and royalty regime.

The state, on the other hand, has no direct financial risk during the exploration phase but it has to monitor that the IOC complies with the work obligations specified in the contract (number of wells to be drilled, depth, technology, etc) and clearly wants any discoveries to be developed as quickly as possible (to boost government coffers). Since the IOC bears the entire exploration risk, it will need to ensure that the contract terms allow for sufficient rewards in the development phase of the project to remunerate these costs and risks. If the contract never enters into its production stage, the IOC will not be able to recover its exploration costs. If commerciality is declared and production begins, the IOC will want to recover its costs as early as possible.

During the development and production stage, apart from the reservoir risk, IOCs face additional uncertainties: the risk of cost increases, and price decreases.

Higher costs can be recovered through the cost recovery mechanism and, in circumstances where uplift arrangements are in place, the impact of higher costs on project value and returns can be minimal to the investor but not to the host government.

Governments like higher investment but dislike higher costs. Price risk refers to sudden significant changes in oil price. A low-price environment may result in the non-exploration of some oilfields, and the non-commerciality of existing operations. The level of price risk to the stakeholders (with the exception of risk service contracts where the government decides to take all the price risk) depends on the extent to which the contract is flexible to accommodate price changes. One of the consequences of the era of high prices and runaway costs is a move towards revenue-based taxation which leaves the risk of cost increase with investors but links production tax and/or royalty rates to oil prices.

Risk service and buyback contracts work in a fundamentally different way.

The investor normally has no price risk or volume exposure but is expected to take development cost exposure. This is asymmetric. Normally, higher oil prices result in higher development costs, hence under risk service contract the investor is exposed to cost inflation risk but gets no compensatory outcomes from the price upside or reservoir performance. This is an additional reason why most IOCs try to avoid risk service agreements. Such contracts seem to function best in respect of managing investment in existing and mature fields, where the investor is taking less risk (no exploration risk, little development risk, extensive subsurface database), rather than in new fields. [1]

6. Arctic exploration
6.1. Basin Analysis
1. For any region, charts and increasingly available digital data and maps derived from them provide the bathymetry and sediment distribution. In the Arctic, the primary frame of

---

[1] Philip Daniel, Michael Keen and Charles McPherson: The Taxation of Petroleum and Minerals. international Monetary Fund. 2010. P 115: 117

reference is Jakobsson et al. (2004, 2008). The amount of information available varies considerably from place to place. For instance, in the GoM, where decades of exploration and drilling has yielded immense datasets and publications, very detailed numerical analysis such as that undertaken by Frye (2008) can be accomplished. In the Arctic, however, data is much sparser and studies of that type require new surveys.

At the basic level, only enough information needs to be accessed to allow for the general geological framework and distribution of erosional-depositional environments to be understood. Although bathymetry and seafloor conditions are also important in conventional hydrocarbon exploration (where they are important for drilling strategy), bathymetry and seafloor temperature and pressure are critical to the thickness of the GHSZ below the seafloor. This information is available in the GoM, whereas it is not widely available in the Arctic.

In the absence of detailed geothermal information, the base of the GHSZ may be established empirically from reflection seismic data. NGH exploration in the GoM points the way toward what must be accomplished in the Arctic.

2. Geological basin analysis in the GoM has been conducted in detail as part of conventional

hydrocarbon exploration, including evaluation of stratigraphy and sequence stratigraphy to establish the possibility of beds having primary porosity or secondary porosity zones that could host NGH concentrations.

This evaluation is comparable to the current practice of conventional early stage reservoir analysis. The objective is to locate turbidite depositional systems that would bring sands into the basin. Considerable work bearing on this phase was part of conventional hydrocarbon exploration for deeper objectives, and thus was available and could be directly applied. Similar seismic exploration techniques are being used to localize deep water sand bodies in the North Atlantic. Dmitrieva et al. (2012) for instance, demonstrate their identification of sand-turbidite systems on Paleocene continental slopes and basins between the Shetlands and Norway. Where similar bodies of deep water sands occur within GHSZs, they are prospective for NGH concentrations.

3. Evidence for the presence of subjacent gas and groundwater access to and through the GHSZ was updated and compiled from the gas seeps and vents that are common in the GoM. Ideally, NGH-mineralizing solutions must be able to transit into the GHSZ to attain the greatest likelihood of high-grade NGH concentrations. This information is well known

Petroleum Exploration

to the oceanographic and exploration community and required only analysis from the perspective of NGH.

4. Using geothermal gradient data and seafloor temperature, the base of the GHSZ was identified as a function of water depth and distance from the shore. The GHSZ thickness in the GoM is highly variable owing to the presence of salt diapirs that have a high thermal conductivity. This yields a thickness map that resembles an irregular polka dot quilt. There have been no reports of large salt masses in the Arctic Ocean Basin. Hence, GHSZ thicknesses should be less variable, which is an aid to exploration. Although determining the top and base of the GHSZ is now a common Deepwater practice for seafloor safety and drilling concerns, determining the base of the GHSZ is specific to the exploration for NGH.

5. The top of the GHSZ below the sulfate-natural gas transition zone was determined as part of the geotechnical study of the seafloor as part of the standard drilling safety requirements.

6.2. Potential Reservoir Localization

1. Finer-grained structural contour maps of sands with the acoustic physical properties associated with various degrees of NGH saturation were identified. In addition to the top and bottom of the NGH being identified on the scale of drilling targets, gas-rich zones below

NGH in the sand were also identified. Seismic data was used to create digital structural contour maps on porous bed bases and tops. This procedure is similar to current practices being used to define potential conventional drilling targets.

Existing computer analysis techniques can be directly applied using numerical estimates for NGH saturation of the sands using industry-standard workstations and one of a number of commercial software programs.

2. Isopach maps of strata having the potential to host the NGH were produced to guide drilling. This is also similar to current practices and defines 'reservoir' potential.

3. Other higher frequency, seismic reflection data were obtained. This was similar to industry practices for conventional hydrocarbons, especially for shallow hazard identification.

4. The more detailed geological host information with more precise velocity information was applied. This was the last step to preparation of a drilling plan.

6.3. Deposit Characterization and Valuation

Everything else, such as logging, sampling, reserve calculations, extraction modeling, among other direct sampling and measurements, follows as a result of drilling.

However, the set of economic considerations are very different from valuing a conventional deposit. For instance, conventional deposits tend to be hydrostatic within a reservoir. That is, porosity may vary but whatever porosity there is will be fully filled with gas or petroleum in a mature deposit. Whether NGH forms in bulk, that is, unsupported and entirely within pore water, or affixed to a surface, it is a solid whose formation increases sediment strength and the bulk modulus. NGH values can be expected to vary within a mineralized bed in much the same way that low temperature strata-bound metalliferous mineral deposits do. Economic geological methods for estimating grade, reserves, and value are required to be used rather than conventional liquid and gas methods for the most accurate volumetric assessment. [1]

The first step an oil company will undertake in hydrocarbon exploration and production is to decide what regions of the world are of interest. This will involve evaluating the technical, political, economic, social and environmental aspects of regions under

---

[1] Michael D. Max · Arthur H. Johnson William P. Dillon: Natural Gas Hydrate – Arctic Ocean Deepwater Resource Potential. 2013. P 57: 59

consideration. Technical aspects will include the potential size of hydrocarbons to be found and produced in the region, which will involve scouting studies using publicly available information or commissioning regional reviews, and a consideration of the technical challenges facing exploration and production, for example in very deep offshore waters.

Political and economic considerations include political regime and Government stability, the potential for nationalization of the oil and gas industry, current embargoes, fiscal stability and levels of taxation, constraints on repatriation of profits, personnel security, local costs, inflation and exchange rate forecasts. Social considerations will include any threat of civil disorder, the availability of local skilled workforce and local training required, the degree of effort which will be required to set up a local presence and positively engage the indigenous people. The company will also consider the precautions needed to protect the environment from harm during operations, and any specific local legislation. There may also be a reputational issue to consider when doing business in a country whose political or social regime does not meet with the approval of the company's home Government or shareholders.

Finally, an analysis of the competition will indicate whether the company has any advantage. It may be that if the company has an existing presence in-country from another business interest, such as downstream refining or distribution, the experience from these areas could be leveraged.

Some 90% of the world's oil and gas reserves are owned and operated by National Oil Companies (NOCs), such as Saudi Aramco (Saudi Arabia), Petronas (Malaysia), Pemex (Mexico). For an independent oil company to take a direct share of exploration, development and production activities in a country, it first needs to develop a suitable agreement with the Government, often represented by the NOC.

The invitation to participate may be publicly announced, in the form of a licensing round. Alternatively, an arrangement for participation may be privately agreed with the NOC. In order to gain an advantageous position on this process, an oil company will expend effort to understand the local conditions, often by setting up a small presence in-country through which relationships are formed with key Government representatives such as the Oil and Gas Ministry, Department of Environmental Affairs and local authorities.

The understanding of local conditions and the requirements of the country, along with the relationships built, may result in a direct agreement for participation in the country or at least an advantageous position when a public bidding round occurs. The investment made during the Gaining Access phase may be considerable, especially in terms of time and the commitment of representatives – it may take a decade of setting up the groundwork before any tangible results are seen, but this is part of the investment process of hydrocarbon exploration and production. [1]

For more than century petroleum geologists have been looking for oil. During this period major discoveries have been made in many parts of the world.

However, it is becoming increasingly likely that most of the 'giant' fields have already been discovered and that future finds are likely to be smaller, more complex, fields.

This is particularly true for mature areas like the North Sea and the shallow water Gulf of Mexico (GoM).

Fortunately, the development of new exploration techniques has improved geologists' understanding and increased the efficiency of exploration. So, although targets are getting smaller, exploration and appraisal wells can now

---

[1] Frank Jahn, Mark Cook and Mark Graham: HYDROCARBON EXPLORATION AND PRODUCTION. 2ND EDITION. Elsevier B.V. 2008. P 1: 2

be sited more accurately and with greater chance of success.

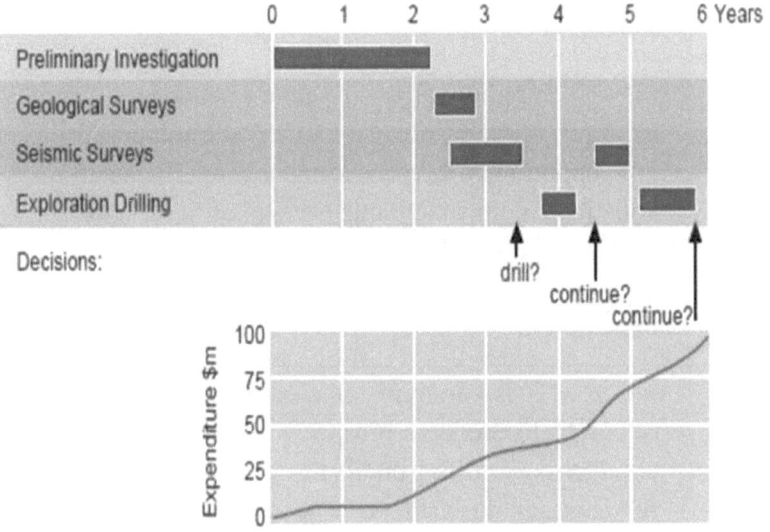

Despite such improvements, exploration remains a high-risk activity. Many international oil and gas companies have large portfolios of exploration interests, each with their own geological and fiscal characteristics and with differing probabilities of finding oil or gas. Managing such exploration assets and associated operations in many countries represents a major task.

Even if geological conditions for the presence of hydrocarbons are promising, host country political and fiscal conditions must also be favorable for the commercial success of exploration ventures. Distance to potential markets, existence of an infrastructure and availability of a skilled workforce are further parameters which need to be evaluated before a long-term commitment can be made.

Traditionally, investments in exploration are made many years before there is any opportunity of producing the oil. In such situations companies must have at least one scenario in which the potential rewards from eventual production justify investment in exploration.

It is common for a company to work for several years on a prospective area before an exploration well is 'spudded' – an industry term for starting to drill. During this period the geological history of the area will be studied and the likelihood of hydrocarbons being present quantified. Prior to spudding the first well a work program will have to be carried out. Field work, magnetic surveys, gravity surveys and seismic surveys are the traditional tools employed. [1]

7. Exploration and Development

Exploration for oil and gas begins with several kinds of geological and geophysical

---

[1] Frank Jahn, Mark Cook and Mark Graham: HYDROCARBON EXPLORATION AND PRODUCTION. 2ND EDITION. Elsevier B.V. 2008. P 2: 3

Petroleum Exploration

surveys. Seismic surveys have turned out to be the most useful. However, exploration and reservoir development remain a challenging stage in the petroleum industry in terms of economics and technology. This stage requires more integrated seismic programs, advanced data analysis systems, and sophisticated operational techniques. Examples of new technologies in

Capital and Exploration Expenditures of the Major Oil Companies (Million U.S. Dollars), 1980–2010[a]

Company	1980	1985	1990	1995	2000	2005	2010
BP	7,409	9,617	9,844	8,380	11,171	14,149	23,016
Upstream	5,018	6,656	5,592	5,261	6,853	10,398	17,753
Downstream	1,964	2,079	3,271	2,989	3,959	2,859	4,029
ExxonMobil	11,565	13,525	11,988	12,862	11,168	17,699	32,226
Upstream	6,974	9,167	6,273	6,986	6,973	14,470	27,319
Downstream	2,830	2,924	4,504	4,724	4,086	3,149	4,720
Total	n.a.	1,679	3,933	2,544	7,677	13,928	21,573
Upstream	n.a.	1,206	1,172	1,294	5,191	10,091	17,510
Downstream	n.a.	305	2,470	1,196	2,217	3,600	3,956
Royal Dutch/Shell	7,959	7,334	9,360	10,965	6,209	15,916	26,940
Upstream	4,974	5,021	3,736	4,477	2,292	4,770	4,523
Downstream	2,498	2,042	4,875	6,163	2,292	4,770	4,523
Chevron	6,674	6,859	7,679	7,928	9,520	11,063	21,755
Upstream	4,273	4,902	4,243	4,651	6,251	8,301	18,904
Downstream	1,302	1,201	3,097	3,075	2,226	2,301	2,552
Total Majors	33,603	39,014	42,804	42,709	45,745	72,755	125,510
Upstream	21,244	26,952	21,016	22,669	28,559	54,206	103,809
Downstream	8,594	8,551	18,226	18,142	14,855	16,666	19,780

[a] Capital and exploration expenditures include upstream, downstream, and other business corporate.

exploration and production (E&P) are 3-D and 4-D seismic imaging, basin modeling, remote sensing integration, and slim-hole drilling. These technical improvements are aimed at reducing the costs of E&P and increasing efficiency with less environmental impact.

Drilling a test well is the necessary next step, to ensure the presence of oil. Drilling methods vary from one area to another. Rotary drilling is more popular in the West; triple drilling is generally used in the former Soviet Union. Drilling is a very expensive operation. Table 2.1 gives the capital and exploration expenditures by major oil companies in 1980, 1985, 1990, 1995, 2000, 2005, and 2010.

The cost of exploration and production by major oil companies has increased over the last three decades by more than 400 percent. This is due mainly to expansion of the oil exploration and production activities beyond the traditional areas to new regions such as Africa and Asia Pacific. In addition to the monopolistic nature of the oil industry, capital and exploration expenditure has increased as a result of the high price of new technologies and the shortage of skilled human resources. Given its high production level and number of wells drilled, the United States accounts for more than 30 percent of world capital and exploratory expenditure. Its cost per well drilled was estimated to be $2 million in 2006, while the cost in Western Europe is almost 10 times higher because of offshore drilling.

One of the reasons drilling is expensive is that in addition to drilling a test well, more confirmation wells have to be drilled near the discovery well to confirm the amount of oil present. Development comes next, when commercial discovery is demonstrated. The process of development consists first in identifying the field based on its geological structure, then drilling development wells, and then establishing gathering systems and other necessary facilities.

From a market structure point of view, oil prices are directly related to the cost of exploration and development. However, rising oil prices since the 1970s stimulated more investment in exploration, even in relatively high-cost areas such as the North Sea and Alaska. This can be seen in Table 2.2, which shows total world exploratory well completions compared to Organization of the Petroleum Exporting Countries (OPEC). The number of wells has

Wells Completed in OPEC Member Countries and in the World, 1980-2010ª

Country	1980	1985	1990	1995	2000	2005	2010
Algeria	249	40	80	95	137	198	258
Angola	24	59	60	60	40	45	118
Ecuador	29	22	38	72	48	131	176
Iran	25	50	24	67	150	183	186
Iraq	67	60	113	10	14	15	71
Kuwait	36	12	7	45	138	67	185
Libya	192	65	98	88	109	115	200
Nigeria	114	64	80	119	85	95	94
Qatar	57	13	23	30	66	62	35
Saudi Arabia	223	96	98	187	257	373	386
United Arab Emirates	109	208	75	112	87	109	146
Venezuela	819	373	236	550	691	1,281	890
Total OPEC	1,998	1,063	932	1,455	1,862	2,690	2,820
World[b]	84,192	91,654	50,880	52,242	60,095	97,430	97,140

increased by 30 percent over the period 1980 to 2010. However, as oil prices decline, the total number of exploratory well completions begin to fall. [1]

In exploration economics, we must consider exploration failure – the possibility of spending funds with no future returns. A typical worldwide success rate for rank exploration

---

[1] Hussein K. Abdel-Aal, Mohammed A. Alsahlawi: Petroleum Economics and Engineering. Third Edition. Taylor & Francis Group, LLC. 2014. P 22:25

activity (i.e. exploring in an unknown area) is one commercial discovery for every 10 wells drilled. Hence an estimate of the reserves resulting from exploration activity must take into account both the uncertainty in the volume of recoverable hydrocarbons and the risk of finding hydrocarbons.

Recall a typical cumulative probability curve of reserves for an exploration prospect in which the probability of success (POS) is 30%. The 'success' part of the probability axis can be divided into three equal bands, and the average reserves for each band is calculated to provide a low, medium and high estimate of reserves, if there are hydrocarbons present.

From this expectation curve, if there are hydrocarbons present (30% probability), then the low medium and high estimates of reserves are 20, 48 and 100 MMstb. The NPV for the prospect for the low, medium and high reserves can be determined by estimating engineering costs and production forecasts for three cases. This should be

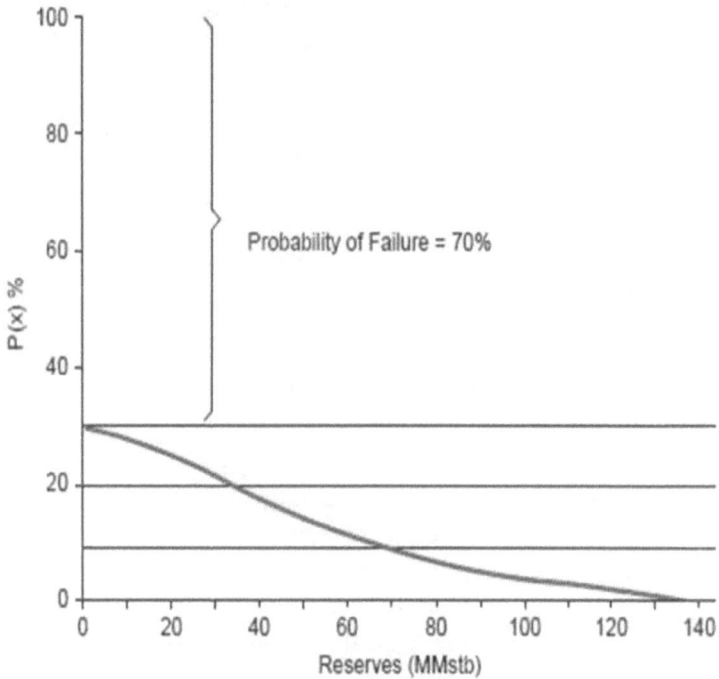

performed not simply by scaling, but by tailoring an engineering solution to each case assuming that we would know the size of reserves before developing the field.

For example, the low case reserves may be developed as a satellite development tied into existing facilities, whereas the high case reserves might be more economic to develop using a dedicated drilling and production facility. We define the EMV of the exploration prospect as

Petroleum Exploration

EMV = Unrisked NPV × POS − PV exploration costs

where POS is the probability of success of an economic development; unrisked NPV is the mean of the H, M, L NPVs (without any consideration of exploration and appraisal costs); PV exploration costs are the discounted cost of the exploration activity.

An alternative way of considering EMV is by presenting the outcomes on a decision tree. The figure is an example of a decision tree which uses the above values.

It is assumed that the cost of the exploration activity is $10 million. The NPV of developing the high, medium and low case reserves are assumed to be $200, $80 and $5 million respectively, so the low case actually makes a loss when taking into account the exploration costs. With an equal probability of low, medium and high cases occurring, and assuming that the low case would be developed to make the small gain, the EMV of the prospect is $85 million, again assuming an exploration cost of $10 million. The above problem has used software from Palisade, called 'Precision Tree'.

In very simple terms, evaluating an exploration opportunity means weighing up the potential prize (multiplied by the probability of winning it) against the certain loss of the exploration cost. The figure is a representation of this risk-reward calculation.

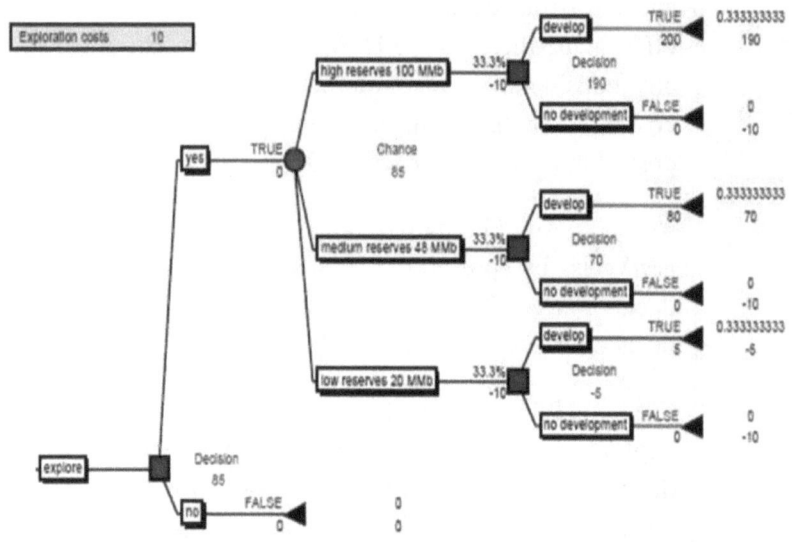

Petroleum Exploration

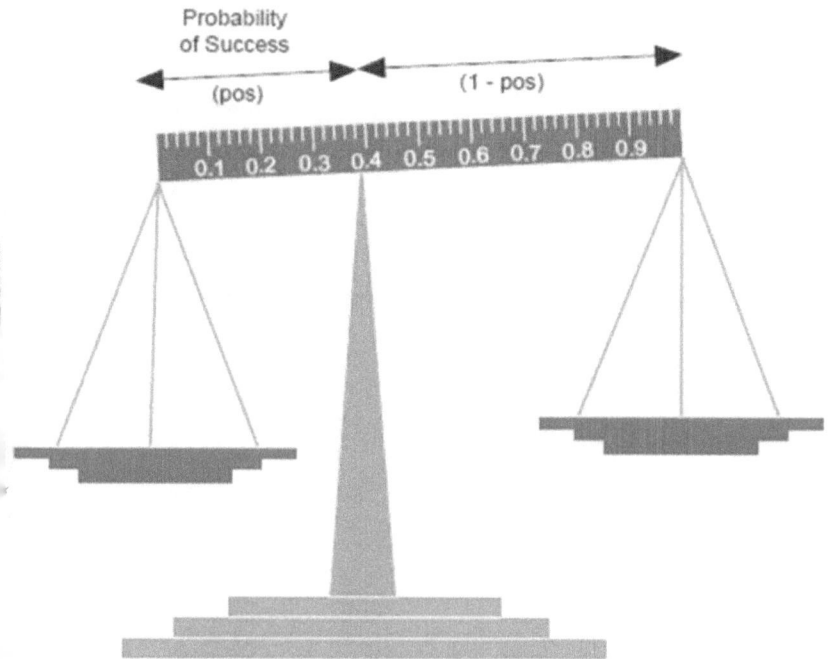

Even if the EMV of an undrilled prospect (after deducting exploration costs) is positive, the investor still needs to determine whether the prospect is significant. For example, would a prospect with an EMV of $50 million be attractive if the exploration cost is $25 million. Such an opportunity would have a 'risk cover' of 2. In other words, one would spend a guaranteed $25 million to win an expected net prize of $50 million. This may not be attractive to investors who have other, better opportunities to pursue. In this case a farm-out may be considered to involve an investor with a different attitude to such risk. [1]

Roshdy Ebrahim

(¹)Frank Jahn, Mark Cook and Mark Graham: HYDROCARBON EXPLORATION AND PRODUCTION. 2ND EDITION. Elsevier B.V. 2008. P 362: 364

References

1. Ali Nezihi Bilge • Ayhan Özgür Toy Mehmet Erdem Günay: Energy Systems and Management. Springer International Publishing Switzerland 2015.
2. Amalia Martı́nez-Garcı́a • Cosme Furlong • Bernardino Barrientos • Ryszard J. Pryputniewicz: Emerging Challenges for Experimental Mechanics in Energy and Environmental Applications, Proceedings of the 5th International Symposium on Experimental Mechanics and 9th Symposium on Optics in Industry (ISEM-SOI), 2015. Springer International Publishing Switzerland 2017.
3. BP Magazine Issue 1. 2015.
4. Chidozie Izuchukwu Princeton Dim: Hydrocarbon Prospectivity in the Eastern Coastal Swamp Depo-belt of the Niger Delta Basin. 2017.
5. Congrui Jin • Gianluca Cusatis: New Frontiers in Oil and Gas Exploration. Springer International Publishing Switzerland 2016.
6. Cyrus Bina: A Prelude to the Foundation of Political Economy. PALGRAVE MACMILLAN. 2013.
7. François Roure • Ammar A. Amin Sami Khomsi • Mansour A.M. Al Garni: Lithosphere Dynamics and Sedimentary Basins of the Arabian Plate and Surrounding Areas. Springer International Publishing AG 2017.
8. Frank Jahn, Mark Cook and Mark Graham: HYDROCARBON EXPLORATION AND

PRODUCTION. 2ND EDITION. Elsevier B.V. 2008.
9. Hussein K. Abdel-Aal Mohamed A. Aggour Mohamed A. Fahim: Petroleum and Gas Field Processing. Second Edition. Taylor & Francis Group, LLC. 2016.
10. Hussein K. Abdel-Aal, Mohammed A. Alsahlawi: Petroleum Economics and Engineering. Third Edition. Taylor & Francis Group, LLC. 2014.
11. Investments in exploration/production and refining 2015. IFP Energies Nouvelles - January 2016.
12. James G. Speight: The Chemistry and Technology of Petroleum. FOURTH EDITION. Taylor & Francis Group, LLC. 2007.
13. Joseph Tawonezvi: The legal and regulatory framework for the EU' shale gas exploration and production regulating public health and environmental impacts. Energ. Ecol. Environ. 2017.
14. K E N N E T H S . D E F F E Y E S: Hubbert's Peak. Princeton University Press. 2001.
15. Khalid Al Hosani • Francois Roure • Richard Ellison • Stephen Lokier: Lithosphere Dynamics and Sedimentary Basins: The Arabian Plate and Analogues. Springer-Verlag Berlin Heidelberg 2013.
16. Michael D. Max · Arthur H. Johnson William P. Dillon: Natural Gas Hydrate – Arctic Ocean Deepwater Resource Potential. 2013.

17. New strategic investments. Al Hilal Publishing and Marketing Group. 2017
18. Nick Snow : Draft leasing program offers 90% of OCS. OGJ Washington. 2018
19. Nuno Luis Madureira: Key Concepts in Energy. Springer International Publishing Switzerland 2014.
20. Oil and gas drive business in the heavy lift sector. Al Hilal Publishing and Marketing Group. 2017
21. Patrick A. Narbel • Jan Petter Hansen Jan R. Lien: Energy Technologies and Economics. Springer International Publishing Switzerland 2014.
22. Philip Daniel, Michael Keen and Charles McPherson: The Taxation of Petroleum and Minerals. international Monetary Fund. 2010.
23. R.L.Sengbush: petroleum exploration, a quantitative introduction, library of congress 1st edition 1986.
24. Rahul Saikia: worth the investment risk. Tank storage magazine. Volume 12, Issue 4.2016.
25. Ripudaman Malhotra: Fossil Energy. Springer Science+Business Media New York 2013.
26. Tank storage magazine: Oil storage opportunities amid Africa's soaring energy demand. Volume 12, Issue 7.2017.
27. Uttam Ray Chaudhuri: Fundamentals of Petroleum and Petrochemical Engineering. Taylor and Francis Group. 2011.
28. Y. Fang . C. Wang . D. Elsworth . T. Ishibashi: Seismicity-permeability coupling in the behavior

Roshdy Ebrahim

of gas shales, CO_2 storage and deep geothermal energy. Springer International Publishing Switzerland 2017.

Biography of the author

Roshdy Ebrahim Abdin, Egyptian.

Ph.D (ECONOMICS)

Economic lecturer.

Member at the Egyptian assembly for political economy.

Member at the Egyptian assembly for international law.

Master degree in economic law.

Professional diploma in arbitration.

Professional diploma in importing and exporting.

Lawyer since 2008.

For more information please subscribe to my blog:

http://roshdyebrahim.blogspot.com.eg/